crime and the punished

the society pages

The Social Side of Politics

Crime and the Punished

Color Lines and Racial Angles (forthcoming)

W. W. Norton & Company has been independent since its founding in 1923, when William Warder Norton and Mary D. Herter Norton first published lectures delivered at the People's Institute, the adult education division of New York City's Cooper Union. The firm soon expanded its program beyond the Institute, publishing books by celebrated academics from America and abroad. By mid-century, the two major pillars of Norton's publishing program—trade books and college texts—were firmly established. In the 1950s, the Norton family transferred control of the company to its employees, and today—with a staff of four hundred and a comparable number of trade, college, and professional titles published each year—W. W. Norton & Company stands as the largest and oldest publishing house owned wholly by its employees.

Book Design: Isaac Tobin
Composition: Westchester Book Composition
Manufacturing: Courier-Westford
Production Manager: Sean Mintus

ISBN: 978-0-393-92038-3

Library of Congress Cataloging-in-Publication Data

Crime and the punished / [edited by] Douglas Hartmann, University of Minnesota, Christopher Uggen, University of Minnesota, Suzy McElrath, University of Minnesota, Sarah Shannon, University of Minnesota.
        pages cm. — (The society pages)
    Includes bibliographical references and index.
    ISBN 978-0-393-92038-3 (pbk.)
    1. Crime—United States.   2. Punishment—United States.   I. Hartmann, Douglas.
    HV6789.C6888   2013
    364.973—dc23

                                                            2013029856

W. W. Norton & Company, Inc., 500 Fifth Avenue, New York, NY 10110-0017
www.wwnorton.com
W. W. Norton & Company, Ltd., Castle House, 75/76 Wells Street, London
W1T3QT

socie
page

crime and the punished

douglas hartmann
UNIVERSITY OF MINNESOTA

christopher uggen
UNIVERSITY OF MINNESOTA

w. w. norton & company
NEW YORK | LONDON

contents

part 3 critical takes

series preface

DOUGLAS HARTMANN AND CHRISTOPHER UGGEN

I t started with a conversation about record labels. Our favorite imprints are known for impeccable taste, creative design, and an eye for both quality and originality. They consistently deliver the best work by the most original voices. Wouldn't it be cool if W. W. Norton & Co. and TheSocietyPages.org joined forces to develop a book series with the same goals in mind?

The Society Pages (TSP) is a multidisciplinary, online hub bringing fresh social scientific knowledge and insight to the broadest public audiences in the most open, accessible, and timely manner possible. The largest, most visible collection of sociological material on the Web (currently drawing about a million hits every month), TSP is composed of a family of prolific blogs and bloggers, podcasts, interviews, exchanges, teaching content, reading recommendations, and original peer-reviewed features. The TSP book series, published in collaboration with W. W. Norton, assembles the best original content from the website in key thematic collections. With contributions from leading scholars, snippets from the site's influential "Community Pages," and a provocative collection of discussion topics and group activities, this innovative series provides an accessible and affordable entry point for strong sociological perspectives on topics of immediate social import and public relevance.

The second volume in this series tackles crime and punishment. As in the first volume, the chapters are organized into three main sections. "Core Contributions" exemplify how sociologists and other social scientists think about otherwise familiar phenomena like crime, incarceration, and suicide. Chapters in the "Cultural Contexts" section engage crime in cultural realms—ranging from politics to families to international crime and justice—that are often ignored or taken for granted. Finally, the "Critical Takes" chapters provide sociological commentary, perspective, and reflections on crime and its control.

Each of these concise, accessible chapters reflects TSP's distinctive tone and style. As with other books in the series, this volume features contributions from TSP Social Facts editor Debby Carr and the Changing Lenses Project. Sprinkled throughout are "TSP Tie-Ins," tying the chapters to content on our website, including Community Pages like Cyborgology, Graphic Sociology, and Lisa Wade and Gwen Sharp's wildly popular and well-respected Sociological Images. The volume concludes with a Discussion Guide and Group Activities that challenge readers to draw connections among the chapters, think more deeply and critically about crime in social life, and link to ongoing conversations and interactive posts online.

introduction

DOUGLAS HARTMANN AND
CHRISTOPHER UGGEN

Last Tuesday night, as Chris powered up his laptop to lecture on "crime as a social construction," he noticed a thin young man in the second row. The student had been badly beaten. Both of his eyes were nearly swollen shut, shadowed by purple-black contusions. He stood unsteadily when approached, saying he'd been robbed and didn't want to miss class—despite a twelve-hour hospital stay. Crime might be a social construction, but it also hurts like hell.

This volume will give you a glimpse into the lived reality that our student and his assailant experienced, but it will also show you how crime and punishment are culturally defined, institutionally structured, and socially negotiated. Sociology is, of course, well known for delving deep into all of the social factors that make the worlds we live in so complicated and problematic. But crime and punishment are especially in need of sociology's insights. We often get so caught up in the raw emotions of crime that we are unable to stand back and analyze it dispassionately. That's why horrific crimes so often lead to laws and punishments that seem extreme (if not horrific) in the cold light of day.

The Society Pages wasn't planning on a "crime volume" this year, but our roundtables, community pages, and white papers fairly pulsed with lively debate and great writing on crime and punishment. Along with our fabulous graduate student board, we were inspired. So, this second volume of the TSP book series with W. W. Norton & Co. selects the best, most engaging, and most timely contributions to our site. We chose the title *Crime and the Punished* because you'll find plenty of data and Durkheimian "social facts" here, but you'll also find interpretation, reflection, and critique that lets you expand your idea of "the punished" to include victims, perpetrators, political institutions, and communities.

As was the case with *The Social Side of Politics*, we have tried to select pieces that will show how the sociological vision and orientation differs from that of other orientations and approaches, particularly those of criminology—the scholarly discipline that is explicitly and unambiguously oriented to explaining crime. In curating our site, working through blog posts, and reviewing and editing submissions, we have learned a lot about what it is that makes the sociological contributions so unique, powerful, and important. A great strength of this volume is that it collects essays on the topics that are the most interesting, important, and timely to the field and to the public. In this respect, we believe it provides an extremely useful entry point to how sociologists think about and research crime and punishment. This volume was helmed by student editors Suzy McElrath and Sarah Shannon, who also wrote the discussion guide.

section-by-section organization

Crime and the Punished is organized in three main sections, each of which highlights distinctive aspects of the sociological vision of crime.

CORE CONTRIBUTIONS

So many student papers begin, "crime is increasing at an alarming rate" that we knew we needed to do some myth-busting. "Six Social Sources of the U.S. Crime Drop," by Christopher Uggen and Suzy McElrath, makes clear that crime has been declining for decades. Changing social interactions, as well as police and prisons, have been a big part of the story. In an interview with Robert Agnew, Sarah Shannon then takes up a new but increasingly urgent threat to declining crime rates: global climate change. Agnew, famous for his "general strain theory," explains how the stresses and strains that cause crime are likely to rise with the temperature. Not everyone will agree with all of Agnew's ideas, but the data he presents are difficult to discount and his is a provocative example of the sociological imagination at work.

Julie Phillips and TSP's Social Facts editor Deborah Carr then take up a timely aspect of a phenomenon that has fascinated sociologists since Durkheim: suicide. Using new statistics, they show how suicide rates still rise sharply during economic recessions. Finally, we couldn't conclude our Core Contributions without engaging the enormous run-up in American incarceration, but even *our* eyes glaze over at the numbers. In "Visualizing Punishment," Shannon and Uggen relate the scale of this increase by telling the story of racialized mass incarceration in maps and pictures.

CULTURAL CONTEXTS

To explain precisely *why* the United States incarcerates its citizens at a greater rate than any other nation, we need an understanding of American political culture. In "Why

Punishment Is Purple," Joshua Page offers a convincing explanation of why the "tough on crime" stance has had such a magnetic bipartisan pull—in turn, he suggests that the political impact and cultural significance of crime and punishment may be even larger than most realize. In tandem with Page's analysis, Jonathan Simon offers cogent commentary on the declining moral legitimacy of mass incarceration, as well as some reasons for cautious optimism about the future.

Although both crime and punishment take place in specific social and cultural contexts, they affect domains that might seem worlds away. In "Repercussions of Incarceration on Close Relationships," Megan Comfort conveys the simple human moments shared between prisoners and their families. She even shows us how visitors assemble birthday cakes from vending-machine ingredients and carefully assemble their outfits so as not to run afoul of prison regulations or metal detectors.

We often take crime, law, and the institutions of justice for granted, but these are constantly recreated as social problems arise (or arise more prominently) on the cultural landscape. Shannon Golden and Hollie Nyseth Brehm address a new era of international criminal justice, gathering four leading experts together for a roundtable on the controversial issues facing criminal courts whose jurisdiction spans borders. Nyseth Brehm concludes the Cultural Contexts section with an affecting analysis of how sociologists are beginning to see the 1994 Rwandan genocide as a million acts of murder, as well as a single historical event.

CRITICAL TAKES

After all this description and explanation of social facts and constructions, we also want to offer a bully pulpit for imagining a different sort of future. What can and should we do to change crime and punishment? Sarah Lageson asked an esteemed roundtable, who were encouraged but not overwhelmed by recent shifts in public opinion. As David Garland put it, "The buildup of the American prison system has taken forty years. It's hard to see how a draw down could take less." But not every "critical take" involves wringing our hands over stubborn inequalities and injustices. There is also an impulse toward progressive reform and social change. In their "A Social Welfare Critique of Contemporary Crime Control," Richard Rosenfeld and Steven Messner ask whether we really want to live in a world of sanitized surveillance, with ever-more intrusive surveillance and controls on our behavior. There are other ways to reduce crime, they argue, that would impose far fewer collateral costs.

When it comes to public policy and social change, academics aren't always the best interpreters or advocates. In "Juvenile Lifers, Learning to Lead," sociologist Michelle Inderbitzin and Oregon State Penitentiary inmates Trevor Walraven and Joshua Cain give us a firsthand perspective on the members of a "lifers club," each of whom received a life sentence while still a teen. Finally, we conclude the volume with another example of "co-production" between academics and those more personally affected by crime and punishment. "Discovering Desistance," by Sarah Shannon and Sarah Lageson, shows how UK criminologists Fergus McNeill and Shadd Maruna worked with former prisoners like Allan Weaver to tell the story of leaving crime behind for good—in their research articles and a powerful new documentary film. We can think of no better or more hopeful conclusion to our crime volume.

As always, we should close with our gratitude to the University of Minnesota, W. W. Norton & Co. (in particular, the sociology editor, Karl Bakeman), and The Society Pages' graduate student board, many of whom are included as authors in this volume. Hollie Nyseth Brehm is our project's graduate editor. Suzy McElrath and Sarah Shannon were the graduate editors of this volume and authored the discussion guide and TSP Tie-Ins found throughout. Our associate editor is the incomparable Letta Page.

changing lenses: we are the 1 in 100

CHRISTOPHER UGGEN

When it comes to crime and punishment, there is no shortage of dramatic visions. We can all conjure pictures of yellow crime scene tape, prison bars, handcuffs, and courtrooms. Yes, there are people in these pictures, but most of us see the uniforms before we see the faces. In crime and justice, social roles are instantly communicated by a distinctive dress code: the police officer's blue uniform, the judge's flowing black robe, and the prisoner's orange jumpsuit (or stripes, for the nostalgic). We hardly notice the human beings wearing the uniforms.

Sometimes we have to create new images just to see past the old ones. We Are the 1 in 100, a project created in Michelle Inderbitzin's sociology class, does just that. The class is part of the Inside-Out Prison Exchange Program, which brings

HOW WOULD YOU LIKE
TO BE JUDGED FOR THE
REST OF YOUR LIFE
BASED ON THE WORST
DECISION YOU EVER
MADE? I AM 1 IN 100

Photo courtesy Trevor Walraven

college students and incarcerated persons together to study as peers inside prison walls. The students in fall 2011 were motivated by a social fact—that 1 of every 100 American adults is incarcerated—and a social movement: the "We are the 99%" cry of the Occupy movement. So, for their class project, they decided to photograph signs that shared their own stories. Each of the students, whether "inside" (serving time in the Oregon State Penitentiary) or "outside" (coming into the prison as Oregon State University undergrads), contributed a statement.

The statements are powerful and challenging:

"My youngest daughter was born 8 months after I was locked-up and I will be out 4 months before she graduates from high school."
"I just got a raise of 25 cents to 35 cents an hour."
"What is my recidivism rate?"

And the images connect us with their authors. Trevor Walraven was both the author and photographer on this image, with fellow inside student "French Fry" holding the sign. It takes courage and trust—and an impressive amount of work, in a ten-week class—to bring these private moments and messages to light, to share and embrace one another's statements as part of your own life, and to capture the idea that punishment is a both an isolating and a social experience.

As Doug Hartmann and Wing Young Huie like to say, the camera lens and the sociological lens reveal different facets of the human experience. Together, the 1 in 100 photographs somehow render the lived reality of prison life in a clear, human, and intimate way.

Read more from Walraven, Inderbitzin, and Cain in this volume's piece "Juvenile Lifers, Learning to Lead." *The* iam1in100.tumblr.com *project welcomes submissions from any person who identifies as the* "1 in 100" *or the many, many more affected by U.S. incarceration.*

core contributions

six social sources
of the u.s. crime drop

CHRISTOPHER UGGEN AND SUZY MCELRATH

ach year, when the federal government releases new crime statistics, reporters seek out crime experts to help interpret the numbers. But following three decades of climbing crime rates, the downward trend of the past two decades has left even the experts searching for answers. Crime dropped under Democrats like Bill Clinton and Barack Obama and when Republicans like George W. Bush were in charge. Crime dropped during times of peace and times of war, in the boom times of the late 1990s and in the Great Recession era from 2007 to 2009. In recent years, both criminologists and the public have been baffled by the improving crime situation—especially when many other social indicators looked so bleak.

But social scientists are starting to make sense of the big U.S. crime drop. At least among many of the "street" crimes reported by police and victims, today's crime rate is roughly half what it was just two decades ago. This isn't because people are twice as nice. Rather, the reasons behind the crime drop involve everything from an aging population to better policing to the rising ubiquity of cell phones. There's no single "smoking gun" that can account for the drop: both formal social controls, such as police and prisons, and broader shifts in the population and economy play a part. That is, the main drivers are all *social.* Crime is less likely these days because of incremental changes in our social lives and interaction with others, including shifts in our institutions, technologies, and cultural practices. Before unpacking these social sources of the crime drop, we need to look a little more closely at its timing and variation across offenses, from auto theft to murder.

dropping like a stone

It might not feel as though the United States is appreciably safer, but both violent and property crimes have dropped steadily and substantially for nearly twenty years. Whether looking to "official" crime (reported to the police) or victimization surveys, the story is the same—both violent and property crimes have dropped like a stone. While crime rose throughout much of the 1960s and '70s, most of today's college freshmen have not experienced a significant rise in the crime rate over the course of their lives.

The Rise and Fall of Crime Rates According to Police

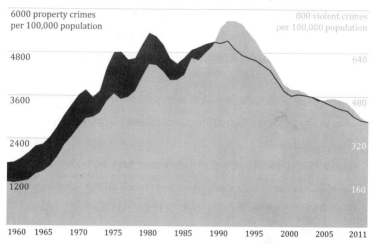

Source: UCR Data Tool, 1960–2010; Crime in the United States, 2011

For all the talk about crime rates (technically, the number of offenses divided by the number of people or households in a given place and time to adjust for population changes), we only have good information about trends for a limited set of offenses—street crimes like murder, rape, robbery, aggravated assault, burglary, theft, auto theft, and arson. Criminologists generally look to two sources of data to measure these crimes: the "official statistics" reported to the police and compiled as "Part I" offenses in the FBI's Uniform Crime Reports and reports from crime victims in the large-scale annual National Crime Victimization Survey. The official statistics are invaluable for understanding changes over time, because the reports have been consistently collected from almost every U.S. jurisdiction over several decades. The victimization data are also invaluable, because they help account for the "dark figure" of crime—offenses that go unreported to the police and are thus missing from the official statistics. Although both speak to the well-being of citizens and their sense of public safety, they do not necessarily show us the whole crime picture (they omit, for example, most white-collar crime and corporate malfeasance). Nevertheless, when victimization data tell the same story as police statistics, criminologists are generally confident that the trend is real rather than a "blip" or a mirage.

First, let's look at the "Part I" crime rate according to the official FBI statistics. Property crimes like burglary and theft are much more common than violent crimes such as rape and robbery (as shown by the larger numbers on the left axis relative to the right axis). Both were clearly rising from the 1960s to about 1980. After some fluctuation in the 1970s and '80s, both rates of reported violence and property crime fell precipitously in 1991. Since then, official statistics show drops of about 49% and 43%, respectively. The sustained drop-off looks even more remarkable when compared to the earlier climb. Official 2011 statistics show offense rates on par with levels last seen in the 1960s for property crimes and in the early '70s for violent crime.

The federal government began taking victimization surveys from a nationally representative sample of households in the 1970s. The victimization picture is clouded by recall errors and other survey methodology challenges, but it's less distorted by unreported crime than the official statistics. Because the survey was redesigned in 1992, we show only the trend in property and violent victimizations from 1993 onward.

Like the official statistics, the victimization data also show a broad-based and long-term crime decline, though there is some evidence of a slight uptick by 2011. There is a drop in violent victimizations through 2009 and a drop in property victimizations through 2010 (apart from a slight rise in 2006 that followed a change in survey methodology). Over this time, violent victimizations fell by 55% (from approximately 50 per 1,000 persons age 12 or older in 1993 to 23 per 1,000 in 2011). Property crimes fell by 57% (from 319 per 1,000 households in 1993 to 139 per 1,000 households in 2011). In both cases, the victim data suggest that the crime drop may be even larger than that suggested by the official statistics.

Declining Property and Violent Victimization

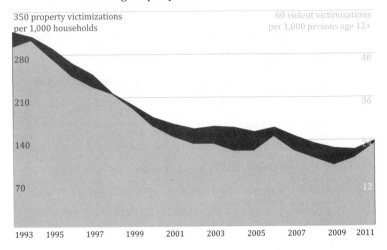

Source: Criminal Victimization, 2009, 2011; Criminal Victimization in the United States series, 1993–2008

It isn't just one type of crime that fell. All seven of the "Part I" offenses reported in the police statistics and the closest corresponding victimization offenses declined by at least 35% from 1993 to 2011. Although the specific offense categories are not directly comparable, similar types of crimes dropped in both the official statistics and the victimization data. For example, the steepest drops occurred for motor vehicle theft, which fell by 62% in official statistics and 74% in the victimization data. Taken together, this provides firm evidence that the crime drop is real, long lasting, and broad in scope.

Drop in Crime and Victimization Rates from 1993 to 2011

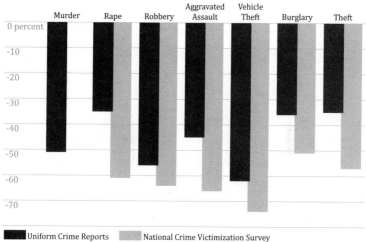

Uniform Crime Reports   National Crime Victimization Survey

Source: UCR Data Tool, 1960–2010; Crime in the United States, 2011; Criminal Victimization, 2009, 2011; Criminal Victimization in the United States series, 1993–2008

six social sources

The big crime drop implies that either fewer people are participating in crime or that those who do participate are committing crime less frequently. But a society's rate of crime is not a simple aggregation of the number of "crime-prone" individuals with particular psychological or biological characteristics. Under the right or, more precisely, the *wrong* social conditions, we are all prone to commit criminal acts. Communities therefore attempt to organize social life in ways that make crime less likely. While we often associate crime with institutions such as the police or courts, anything that alters patterns of human interaction can drive the crime rate up or down. This includes the technology in our cars, the places we go for entertainment, and the medical advances affecting reproduction and aging.

The idea that crime is *social* rather than individual is a prominent theme in much of the best new research. The crime drop partly reflects the work of institutions that are explicitly designed to increase social control, but it also reflects changes in other institutions designed to perform different societal functions.

Scholars have yet to neatly partition the unique contribution of the six social sources of the crime drop, but we can summarize current thinking about their likely impact.

formal social control and criminal opportunities

1. Punishment

No discussion of recent U.S. crime trends would be complete without considering our nation's prison population, which increased from 241,000 in 1975 to 773,000 in 1990 to over 1.6 million in 2010. Because incarceration rose so rapidly, it is tempting to attribute the lion's share of the crime drop to the incapacitating effects of prison. But if this were the case, as law professor Franklin Zimring points out, we should have seen an earlier crime drop (when incarceration first boomed in the 1970s). Instead, because crime is closely tied to the demography of the life course, new cohorts of potential offenders are always replacing those removed via incarceration. Moreover, many criminologists believe that prisons are actually *criminogenic* in the long run, strengthening criminal ties and disrupting noncriminal opportunities when inmates are released.

In one of the most sophisticated studies of the effect of imprisonment on crime, sociologist Bruce Western estimates that roughly nine tenths of the crime drop during the 1990s would have occurred without any changes in imprisonment. Economist Steven Levitt attributes up to one third of the total decline to incarceration. Rising rates of imprisonment thus account for at least some of the crime drop in the 1990s and 2000s, with scholars attributing anywhere from 10 to 30% of the decline to America's incarceration boom.

2. Policing

Both public and private policing strategies have changed considerably over the past several decades, as have the technologies available to law enforcement. Zimring and others conclude that "cops matter," especially in explaining New

York City's crime decline. More specifically, criminologists David Weisburd and Cody Telep identify targeted policing of high-crime "hot spots," gun crimes, and high-rate offenders, as well as proactive problem-oriented policing and the use of DNA evidence as police practices that reduce crime. In contrast, they find little evidence for the effectiveness of policing tactics like random preventive patrol, follow-up visits in domestic violence cases, and Drug Abuse Resistance Education (the D.A.R.E. program).

While Levitt is skeptical about the role of new policing strategies, he attributes a portion of the 1990s crime drop to increases in the number of officers on the street. Because of the criminogenic effects of prison, scholars such as economist Steven Durlauf and criminologist Daniel Nagin propose shifting a greater share of criminal justice funding in policing. Effective law enforcement is part of the picture, says criminologist John MacDonald, but he also argues that public-private security partnerships such as targeted "business improvement districts" have helped to sustain the decline. The unique contribution of policing to the current crime drop is likely significant, but limited—accounting for perhaps 10 to 20% of the overall decline. Moreover, the effectiveness of the formal social controls provided by police depends, in large part, on support from informal social controls provided by families and communities.

3. Opportunities

Apart from changes in prisons and policing, the *opportunities* for crime have changed rapidly and dramatically since the 1990s. Technology isn't an obvious social source of the crime drop, but people have been connecting in fundamentally different ways in the past two decades, altering the risks and rewards of criminal behavior. When it comes to "target hardening" (crime prevention through environmental design), simple changes can make an enormous difference. Recall that the biggest drop among all crime categories was in auto theft—in the United States and around the world, new technologies like car immobilizers, alarms, and central locking and tracking devices have effectively reduced this crime.

More generally, surveillance provides guardianship over ourselves and our property. It may even deter others from acting against us. With regard to a now-common technology, economists Jonathan Klick and Thomas Stratmann and criminologist John MacDonald point to the amazing proliferation of cell phones. They argue that cells increase surveillance and a would-be offender's risk of apprehension, which affects the perceived costs of crime. Many potential victims now have easy access to a camera and are within a few finger swipes of a call to 9-1-1. In a follow-up interview with the authors about his research, MacDonald said that the crime drop is "driven in part by target hardening, in part by consumer technological shifts, and in part by the movement of people's nighttime activities back to the house." In sum, where we spend our time and who is watching us likely plays a big role in the recent crime decline.

Of course, efforts to constrain criminal opportunities can also constrain noncriminal activities—and while most of us welcome the declining crime rates that accompany greater surveillance, we are far more ambivalent about being watched ourselves. As criminologist Eric Baumer explained to the authors, "not only are we spending more time off the streets and on a computer, but we are being watched or otherwise connected to some form of 'social control' pretty constantly when we are out and about." It is difficult to quantify how myriad small changes in criminal opportunities affected the crime drop, but their *combined* contribution may be on a par with that of formal policing or prisons.

social trends and institutional change

4. Economics

More than 90% of the "Part I" crimes reported to the police involve some kind of financial gain. The relationship between crime and the economy is more complicated than the simple idea that people "turn to crime" when times are tough, though. Contrary to popular expectations, for example, both victimizations and official crime showed especially steep *declines* from 2007 to 2009, when unemployment rates soared. Robbery, burglary, and household theft victimizations had been falling by a rate of about 4% per year from 1993 to 2006, but fell by an average of 6 to 7% per year during the Great Recession.

This is not because crime is unrelated to economic conditions but because crime is related to so many other things. For example, when people have less disposable income, they may spend more time in the relative safety of their home and less time in riskier places like bars. As noted above regarding opportunities, another reason crime rates are likely to drop when cash-strapped residents stay home at night in front of a television or computer screen is that their mere presence can help prevent burglary and theft.

Criminologists Richard Rosenfeld and Robert Fornango suggest that consumer confidence and the *perception* of economic hardship may account for as much as one third of the recent reduction in robbery and property crime. Nevertheless, while economic recessions and consumer sentiment are likely to play some role, they cannot account for the long and steady declines shown in the charts above—boom or bust, crime rates have been dropping for twenty years. For this reason, most criminologists attribute only a small share of the crime drop to economic conditions.

5. Demography

Crime, it seems, is largely a young man's game. For most offenses, crime and arrests peak in the late teen years and early twenties, declining quickly thereafter. During the 1960s and 1970s, the large number of teens and young adults in the Baby Boom cohort drove crime rates higher. In societies that are growing older, such as the contemporary United States, there are simply fewer of the young men who make up the majority of criminal offenders and victims. Due to these life course processes, the age and gender composition of a society is an underlying factor that structures its rate of crime.

An influx of new immigrants might also be contributing to lower crime rates. According to research by sociologist Robert Sampson and his colleagues, immigration can be "protective" against crime, with first-generation immigrants being significantly less likely to commit violence than third-generation Americans, after adjusting for personal and neighborhood characteristics.

While criminologists estimate that demographic changes can account for perhaps 10% of the recent crime drop, these factors are changing too slowly to explain why crime was essentially halved within the course of a single generation.

6. Longer-Term Social Dynamics

Drawing back the historical curtain on U.S. crime rates puts the recent drop in perspective. So argued historian Eric Monkkonen, who showed that the urban homicide rates of the nineteenth and early twentieth centuries were on a par with the "peak" rates observed in the early 1990s. In fact, historical evidence amassed by scholars including psychologist Steven Pinker and historical criminologist Manuel Eisner convincingly shows that personal violent crime began declining in Western nations as early as the sixteenth century. While this research has emphasized violent crimes, similar processes may hold for crime more generally. Perhaps the rising crime rate from World War II through the early 1990s was simply a small spike that temporarily obscured a much longer downward trend.

This long historical sweep may offer little solace to those confronted by crime today, but the encouraging long-term trend suggests explanations with deep roots. Eisner points to subtle shifts in parenting occurring over a long time span; Pinker suggests greater interdependence and broadened circles of people with whom we can empathize. Both draw on classic sociological work by Emile Durkheim and Norbert Elias, who attributed historical changes in crime and social disorder to changes in the relation between individuals and society. The centuries-long crime story is perhaps best explained by the gradual development of formal and informal social controls on our behavior. In this light, Baumer argues that we should at least think more expansively about the contemporary crime drop. We cannot say for certain where the crime rate will be in five years, but if we had to bet where the crime rate would be in *one hundred* years, we could be reasonably confident it'd be measurably lower than it is today.

room for improvement

Criminologists almost universally acknowledge a sizeable crime drop over the last twenty years. This does not mean that everyone's neighborhood became safer or that crime in the United States is low relative to other industrialized nations. In fact, U.S. homicide rates are more than double those of Canada, Japan, and much of Europe. Nevertheless, the U.S. crime picture has improved markedly, with significant across-the-board drops in violent and property offenses. Moreover, as Baumer points out, even behaviors like drinking, drug use, and risky sex are declining, especially among young people.

We cannot explain such a sharp decline without reference to the social institutions, conditions, and practices shaping crime and its control. In particular, social scientists point to punishment, policing, opportunities, economics, demography, and history, though there is little consensus about the relative contribution of each. Further disentangling each factor's unique contribution is a worthy endeavor, but it should not obscure a fundamental point: it is their entanglement in our social world that reduces crime.

RECOMMENDED READING

Eric P. Baumer and Kevin Wolff. 2012. "Evaluating the Contemporary Crime Drop(s) in America, New York City, and Many Other Places," *Justice Quarterly* 1–34. An up-to-the-minute appraisal of explanations for local, national, and global crime trends.

Manuel Eisner. 2003. "Long-Term Historical Trends in Violent Crime," *Crime and Justice* 30:83. A rich treatment of the decline in European homicide rates from the sixteenth to twentieth centuries.

Steven D. Levitt. 2004. "Understanding Why Crime Fell in the 1990s: Four Factors That Explain the Decline and Six That Do Not," *Journal of Economic Perspectives* 18(1):163–190. A systematic appraisal of explanations for the crime decline by the renowned economist and *Freakonomics* author.

Eric H. Monkkonen. 2002. "Homicide in New York, Los Angeles, and Chicago," *Journal of Criminal Law and Criminology*

92(3):809–822. A careful historical examination of homicide in the nineteenth and twentieth centuries.

Franklin E. Zimring. 2007. *The Great American Crime Decline,* New York: Oxford University Press. A well-written and thorough account of the U.S. crime drop.

climate change and crime with robert agnew

SARAH SHANNON

With growing attention to climate change, environmental protection laws are on the rise around the globe. Green criminology has emerged as an area of study focused on how laws designed to safeguard the environment, humans, and animals are violated by governments, corporations, militaries, and ordinary people. Green criminologists study how damage done intentionally or through negligence creates other harms, such as pollution, deforestation, species decline, and bio-piracy. Like other criminologists, those who study environmental crime study who commits the crime, who or what is victimized, and the social, economic, and political conditions that lead to environmental crimes.

Green criminologists are also interested in how environmental protection laws are made. Recognizing that these laws are socially constructed, green criminologists look beyond how these laws are breached to how they are created in the first place. As with other types of law, inequalities in race, gender, and power influence how environmental protection laws are formed and enforced. From this perspective, environmental crime may or may not break existing environmental protection laws. Green criminologists ask fundamental questions about what types of environmental harms can or should be considered crimes.

Like criminologists in general, green criminologists draw on theories of policing, punishment, and crime prevention to consider how best to respond to environmental harm and develop ideas about social, environmental, and ecological justice.

Robert Agnew, a criminologist famous for his development of the general strain theory of crime, wrote an article called "Dire Forecast: A Theoretical Model of the Impact of Climate Change on Crime" (2012) that discusses how climate change and crime might go hand in hand. In this essay, based on an Office Hours podcast interview with Sarah Shannon, Agnew explains why he thinks climate change may become one of the biggest drivers behind rising crime rates in the twenty-first century. To listen to the full podcast discussion with Agnew, visit thesocietypages.org /crime.

connecting climate change and crime

I've been a criminologist for several decades now, but I've also had a personal interest in climate change since the mid-1990s. With each passing year, I became more and more concerned about climate change and what it might bring. As the science has become more certain, and as forecasts have become more dire, I've really begun to feel almost something of a moral obligation: this is, perhaps, the greatest crisis that will confront humanity. I need to something about it. It occurred to me that my particular strength is academic research—maybe there's something I can do in that area to make the greatest contribution.

As I began to look at the literature on climate change, I noticed initially that the predictions focused on just the physical impact of climate change, but more and more, social and behavioral scientists were getting involved. Some political scientists, for example, were talking about the possible impact of climate change on social conflict; public health researchers talked about the impact on health; and others talked about the impact on migration. It occurred to me that there's good reason to think that climate change might also have an impact on crime.

This isn't something that criminologists have devoted much attention to, although I might mention that an emerging area in the field of criminology is known as "green" or "environmental criminology," but there wasn't really much discussion about how climate change might impact crime. Since most of the work I do in criminology focuses on the causes of crime, I decided to take my emerging knowledge of climate change, combine it with my knowledge of the causes of crime, and argue that there's good reason to believe that, if climate change proceeds, it may become one of the major forces—if not the major force—driving crime.

climate change 101

Climate change is being driven by an increase in heat-trapping gases in the atmosphere, principally carbon dioxide, but also other gases like methane. We're quite certain that this increase is largely due to human activities, especially the burning of fossil fuels, and to a lesser extent deforestation.

Climate change itself involves several related phenomena. It will involve, among other things, a rise in average temperature (and this is already happening, this isn't the future). Twelve of the warmest years on record have occurred in the last thirteen years. If you've been listening to the news lately, even up north we're setting a lot of record temperatures. A few decades ago, the ratio of record highs to record lows was about 1:1, but recently the ratio has changed to about 2:1. The average annual temperature in the United States has increased by more than two degrees Fahrenheit over the last fifty years, with close to a five-to-seven-degree Fahrenheit increase in Alaska and western Canada. Most scientists agree that anything more than a two-degree Celsius increase will bring catastrophic results; right now, we're expecting maybe a four-to-five-degree increase by the end of the century, if not sooner.

In addition to a rise in average temperature, climate change will bring changing patterns of precipitation. It will get warmer, sea level will rise, and there will be an increase in extreme weather events: heat waves, droughts, cyclones, hurricanes, floods. For example, the 2003 European heat wave killed over seventy thousand people, including fifteen thousand or more in France, where temperatures reached 104 degrees Fahrenheit. Melting glaciers in the Alps caused flooding in Switzerland. Over 5% of the total forest area in Portugal burned. There was a 30% drop in plant productivity due to drought. In the last year or so, there have been numerous instances of drought, heat waves, and flooding in China, Pakistan, Russia, Australia, the horn of Africa, and here in the United States.

These are some of the phenomena associated with climate change, and they are going to have a number of effects that,

I argue, will directly and indirectly increase crime. Climate change will impose heightened economic demands on nations that are not prepared to meet that challenge. For example, things like rising temperature, rising sea level, and extreme weather events will damage infrastructure—roads, bridges, pipelines, power lines, water sanitation facilities—and many nations will not be able to recover afterward. It will hurt their economic development and contribute to poor health outcomes, transportation problems, you name it. Many countries will not have the economic resources to adapt to and recover from climate change.

Drought will force people off the land, sea-level rise will force coastal inhabitants to move, social conflict might force many to flee to safer areas, and extreme weather events and forest fires will destroy homes and livelihoods. Some estimates say that, by mid-century, we may have literally hundreds of millions of environmental migrants, though the estimates in this area vary a lot. There's little doubt that climate change will dramatically increase migration across borders and within countries, and that it'll increase social conflict with competition over scarce resources—competition among nations, and also competition among groups within nations. Migration produced by climate change will foster social conflict especially when migrants move to areas where resources are scarce and where there are preexisting social divisions between the migrants and the people in the receiving area. Climate change will weaken states.

In short, climate change will set off a number of major physical, economic, health, and social effects. Many of these effects may impact causes of crime in ways that increase the likelihood of crime.

climate, strain, and crime

There's good evidence that certain strains or stressors increase the likelihood of crime. Not all strains or stressors, but those that are high in magnitude, those that are seen as unjust, and those that have certain other characteristics. And people who experience these strains or stresses, among other things, experience a range of negative emotions. They become upset, angry, frustrated, depressed, and so on, and that creates pressure to take corrective action. You feel bad, you want to do something about it. And one possible response—certainly not the only one or even the most common—is crime. There's good reason to think that climate change will increase the number of strains or stressors and thereby increase crime. Here are a few examples.

Climate change will result in an uncomfortable increase in temperature, both average temperature and temperature spikes. And there has been some research suggesting that when the temperature rises, particularly when there's a large increase in temperature (past a certain threshold), crime increases, especially violent crime, but perhaps also property crime. There's also some evidence that the effect of temperature is stronger in low-income areas, where access to air conditioning is limited, and rural areas, where outdoor activity is more common. Climate change will increase average temperature, temperature spikes, and heat waves, and there's some research suggesting that, when temperature increases, it may increase crime. In part, this is for reasons related to strain theory. High temperatures makes people angry, irritable, touchy. Also, it may increase crime for reasons related to other theories. When it's warmer, for example, people spend more time outdoors and there's an increased opportunity for crime with more people interacting with one another.

Another example: We know that climate change will increase extreme weather events—floods, hurricanes, droughts—and blackouts will increase as well. These events are not only strains or stressors in and of themselves but they can lead to a host of additional strains: physical injury, death, destruction of home and property, loss of livelihood, and so on. There's been some research on natural disasters and crime, and, interestingly, most of the research suggests that crime, despite popular perception, decreases after a natural disaster. People kind of pull together, they help one another, they take care of one another, but in some cases, crime increases after a natural disaster. This was the case with Hurricane Hugo in St. Croix; Andrew in Homestead, Florida; and Katrina in Louisiana for certain categories of people. The most recent research suggests that natural disasters are more likely to increase crime when disaster victims believe the government will be unable to meet pressing needs for food, water, and shelter; post-disaster problems are blamed on others; security is lax; and there are preexisting divisions or resentments among those in the affected area.

As climate change proceeds, disasters, I argue, will increasingly have these features. They'll become more frequent and severe, straining the ability of people and governments to meet basic needs and provide security; they'll often be blamed on other individuals (as climate change proceeds and as knowledge about climate change grows, people will increasingly realize this isn't an act of nature, an act of God, or a random event, rather it is something that was created by humans); and these natural disasters, I contend, will more often occur in the context of social division. So that's another strain that I feel will increase crime.

Yet another: food and fresh water shortages. It's not unreasonable to suppose these might lead to crimes like theft, aggression (against those blamed for the shortages), and maybe corporate and state crimes (price gouging, forced displacement, etc.) In criminology, there hasn't been a lot of research on the impact of food and fresh water shortage on crime, but there's been some. For example, studies among the homeless suggest that homeless individuals who report that they're particularly hungry are more likely to engage in crime, and certain anecdotal evidence suggests that food and fresh-water shortages might increase crime. When food prices spiked in the mid-2000s, an increase of over 80%, there were riots in thirty countries.

Climate change will increase poverty and inequality. Many people will lose their livelihood because of extreme weather events, sea-level rise, poor health, forced migration, and social conflict. One of the things that we know about climate change, natural disasters, and so on is that they don't affect everyone equally. Not surprisingly, the wealthy people in developed countries are much better able to adapt. They suffer less. And so, natural disaster, among other things, increases inequality, and that exacerbates the effects of poverty. It makes poverty seem all the more serious, all the more unjust. Poverty and inequality are among major causes of crime.

Forced migration, I argue, is another stressor that may increase crime. Immigration in and of itself doesn't seem to increase crime, but, in certain cases it does, and I argue that the immigration that will be associated with climate change will be forced migration. People immigrating will experience a range of stressors: people in the receiving areas may be hostile to immigration, competition over scarce resources, and so on.

Climate change will reduce coping skills and resources. It will rob people of financial and other resources. It will reduce social support. Governments will be less able to provide assistance. You'll be less likely to turn to family, friends, and so on for assistance, because they will be suffering, too.

legal coping strategies

I'm talking about what *might* happen in the future based on what we know about climate change and the predicted effects of climate change, along with theories of crime, and, in some cases, small bodies of research. But, it doesn't *have* to happen.

One way that we can deal with a possibly grim future is to take steps to reduce those actions that contribute to climate change. Unfortunately, if you have been paying attention to the media, you know that we haven't been doing a whole lot in that area. The United Nations, for example, has been sponsoring international conferences on climate change but not much has resulted from those conferences. There are a number of things that we can do, from conservation to promoting green energy to changes in lifestyle, and so on.

Beyond that, we also need to think about adapting to climate change and its effects. Because even if we could somehow magically seesaw carbon emissions tomorrow, it's going to stay in the atmosphere for a long time, and the climate change that has begun will continue. So, we need to think about how to adapt to climate change, and particularly need to help those countries in the developing world and certain groups in all countries (including in the developed world) that will suffer the most from climate change—the poor, women, in some countries certain racial minority groups, the very old, the very young—and help them better adapt. Some cities like Seattle, San Francisco, Chicago, and New York City are developing climate action plans. Not too long ago, for example, there was a major heat wave in Chicago. Many people died, or suffered very badly from it. That's one of the reasons that Chicago is leading the way among U.S. cities to deal with this: they don't want a repeat of that tragedy. Some companies are taking a lot of action in this area too.

There are a number of things we can do both to reduce the extent of climate change and to reduce the likelihood that, as the effects of climate change become more severe, people don't have to go out and turn to crime to get that fresh water and food. Cities or countries can become better prepared to meet their population's needs so that they don't turn to crime.

Fortunately, we're in a situation where we have a pretty good idea of what we need to do. It's not like we desperately need more research, or we don't know how to respond—there are a number of strategies we can take, and there's good reason to believe these strategies will even be cost-effective over the long run.

PARTICIPANT PROFILE

Robert Agnew is a sociologist at Emory University. He is the author of *Pressured Into Crime: An Overview of General Strain Theory*.

RECOMMENDED READING

Robert Agnew. 2006. *Pressured Into Crime: An Overview of General Strain Theory*. New York: Oxford University Press. A theoretically and empirically persuasive argument that strain is intimately linked to criminal behavior.

Robert Agnew. 2012. "Dire Forecast: A Theoretical Model of the Impact of Climate Change on Crime," *Journal of Theoretical*

Criminology. A compelling analysis of how and why climate change might increase crime in the twenty-first century.

Piers Beirne and Nigel South, editors. 2012. *Issues in Green Criminology: Confronting Harms Against Environments, Humanity, and Other Animals*. Portland, OR: Willan. Examines the various ways that governments, transnational corporations, military operations, and ordinary people routinely harm environments, and human and other animal life.

Rob White, editor. 2010. *Global Environmental Harm: Criminological Perspectives*. Portland, OR: Willan Publishing. Presents original, cutting-edge work on global environmental harm from a wide variety of geographical and critical perspectives.

social fact: the great depressions?

DEBORAH CARR AND JULIE A. PHILLIPS

D uring the Great Depression of the late 1920s, suicide rates in the United States reached an all-time high, topping 22 suicides per 100,000 persons. Images of once-wealthy business moguls and industrialists throwing themselves from Manhattan skyscrapers may seem a tragic memory of years past, yet contemporary data show that suicide rates ebb and flow dramatically with ups and downs in the economy—especially for men.

Suicide, or taking one's own life, was the 10th most common cause of death in the United States in 2009, with rates consistently higher for men than women, and whites relative to blacks. Young adults (ages 20–24) have higher suicide rates than children, teenagers, or other adults, yet white men ages 85 and older have the highest suicide rate of any demographic group. In recent years, highly publicized suicides among military veterans and gay and lesbian adolescents

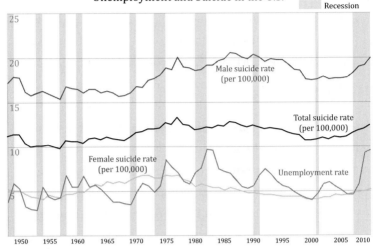

Unemployment and Suicide in the U.S.

Recession

Male suicide rate
(per 100,000)

Total suicide rate
(per 100,000)

Female suicide rate
(per 100,000)

Unemployment rate

Sources: Suicide data from CDC/NCHS, National Vital Statistics System, Mortality; Unemployment data from Bureau of Labor Statistics (http://data.bls.gov/timeseries/LNS14000000)

have called attention to the special stressors facing these subgroups. At an individual level, suicide is influenced by a range of social, psychological, and biological factors, most notably untreated depression. At a population level, however, aggregate-level suicide patterns mirror macroeconomic trends, including unemployment rates and business cycles.

The graphic above shows U.S. unemployment rates and suicide rates among men and women from 1948 to 2011. For men, suicide rates follow patterns that roughly mirror national unemployment rates. Unemployment spiked in the

1970s—a period marked by an oil crisis and stagflation—and again in the "double-dip" recession years of the early '80s. Men's suicide rates also spiked during these periods, and remained quite high throughout the '80s, before dipping during the dot-com boom years in the '90s. During the recession beginning in 2007 and continuing today, unemployment rates have again spiked, and men's suicide rates have followed a similar, although more muted, pattern.

Women's overall suicide rates are consistently lower than men's, averaging close to 5 per 100,000 (vs. roughly 18 per 100,000 among men). Women's rates were highest during a strong economic period: the late 1960s through 1970s. By contrast, during the recessionary periods of the early 1980s and early twenty-first century, women's suicide rates were low and stable.

It is impossible to "prove" whether aggregate-level patterns of economic distress trigger men's suicide or whether individual women's suicides are a response to widespread social and normative unrest like that at play in the late 1960s. However, sociological writings dating back to Emile Durkheim suggest that any social phenomenon that weakens a person's sense of social integration and connectedness or that profoundly undermines feelings of self-worth may trigger depressive symptoms, a common underlying cause of suicide. Stress theories also find that major stressful events, including job loss or home foreclosure, may create a string of "secondary stressors" including marital troubles, residential relocations, and disruptions to one's daily activities and routines. All of these secondary stressors may place one at risk of depression, anxiety, and substance use—all potential triggers of suicidal behaviors. These risks may be particularly acute for men, who are socialized to believe that a man's worth depends on his ability to be his family's "breadwinner." Although publicly funded health initiatives also suffer during lean economic times, suicide prevention and depression treatment programs are all the more critical during times of recession.

TSP tie-in

legalizing marijuana

I n November 2012, citizens in the states of Colorado and Washington voted to legalize the recreational use of marijuana, though ballot initiatives in two other states— California and Oregon—had been voted down in 2010 and 2012, respectively. Public support for legalizing marijuana is at an all-time high and growing, with Gallup polls indicating 44% in favor. As one Sociology Lens post points out, states may even hope to impose new "vice taxes" on marijuana in order to address fiscal shortfalls and fund frequently neglected programs, such as capital improvements for schools or drug treatment. Is legalization of marijuana the trend of the future? If so, what does it mean for crime and punishment policy?

As Katherine Beckett discusses in a Scholars Strategy Network brief featured on The Society Pages, tens of thousands of people have been arrested for violating marijuana laws during the United States' 40-year-long War on Drugs.

The laws' attempt to reduce drug use with tough penalties has been shown ineffective, though. Much research shows that these efforts have failed—at great cost to society, families, and individuals. Enforcing the laws, Beckett writes, is expensive, overloads the criminal justice system, and contributes to racial disparities in arrest rates. Families and individuals also pay high emotional and financial costs for marijuana arrests, whether or not the arrest ultimately leads to conviction.

What about the potential drawbacks of decriminalizing marijuana use? As Chris Uggen explains in one Public Criminology post, there is not a lot of evidence to go on, but the complications and consequences could be substantial. According to one analysis of how legalizing marijuana in California might have changed things, it's clear the cost of marijuana would go down and demand would go up. But other outcomes are harder to pin down: How much money would be generated through taxes? How much would be saved in criminal justice costs? Perhaps more complex, Colorado's and Washington's new laws conflict with national drug laws, in which marijuana is still an illegal, controlled substance. It's not clear how this difference will be resolved.

If nothing else, the new legislation will provide the opportunity to answer such questions, paving the way for future changes at the state and national levels. As one Sociological

Images post reminds us, sociologist Kai Erickson argues that once a society creates institutions and industries to deal with a certain type of deviance, it tends to continuously find enough deviance to justify the system's existence. This is to say, legalizing marijuana might focus our attention only on *new* deviant behaviors that provide reason to continue funneling significant social and economic resources to the criminal justice system.

SARAH SHANNON

visualizing punishment

SARAH SHANNON AND CHRISTOPHER UGGEN

our decades ago, the United States launched a grand
policy experiment. The nation began locking up an
unprecedented share of its citizens, increasing its rate
of incarceration by more than 400% over the period. According to the Bureau of Justice Statistics, the number of U.S.
prisoners finally stabilized in 2009, showing small declines
for the first time since the 1970s. The long-term effects of
this experiment are only beginning to come into focus, but
they are so powerful and so concentrated in communities of
color that scholars such as Michelle Alexander liken mass
incarceration to a "new Jim Crow"—a wide-ranging and
racialized system of social control.

This boom was unparalleled among Western developed
nations. On any given day, about 2 million U.S. citizens are
now behind bars and more than 3 million former prisoners
are contending with labor market discrimination, loss of
voting rights, difficulty securing housing, and problems

reconnecting with family. In some states, as many as 10% of adult African Americans have served prison time. This is not to mention the millions of other "legal bystanders" (to use sociologist Megan Comfort's fine phrase) who come into contact with the criminal justice system through their relationships with its clients.

With a story so big, one might expect mass incarceration to garner regular front-page headlines. One reason it has not received such coverage might be because, until recently at least, there has been little incentive to question this trend. The United States is a wealthy nation and can, by and large, afford the exorbitant expenses incurred by locking up millions of citizens for long periods of time. Only since the Great Recession have states begun to cut back on correctional spending and, in some cases, close facilities due to tight state budgets. A second reason may be that Americans, as legal scholar Michael Tonry and others have pointed out, tend to support punitive policies, especially in reaction to moral panics over particularly egregious crimes. Finally, the relative lack of attention to the punishment boom may be due to its magnitude; its scale is just too immense for most people to grasp. *Millions* of people, *billions* of dollars—it's no wonder even interested eyes glaze over.

Data visualization can begin to address this third point, since a good picture is often worth a thousand statistical tables. Journalists, social scientists, and data gurus such as Hans Rosling are using geographic information systems and other visualization tools to move from "boring" statistics to eye-catching and intuitive images. For example, the *New York Times* and the *Guardian* regularly communicate complicated social issues and trends using attractive maps, tables, and graphs. Our task here is to visualize the story of mass incarceration, illustrating shifts in punishment over time, space, and the populations most affected by its rise.

time

The U.S. incarceration rate was relatively stable throughout most of the twentieth century, fluctuating in a narrow range around 100 per 100,000 people. In the early 1970s, however, its steep climb began. Imprisonment increased by an average of 6% per year to reach its current rate of about 500 per 100,000 people. Over the past few years, incarceration rates have stabilized and even fallen slightly. Still, you can see in the graph below that the nation continues to imprison people at five times the rate it did in the early 1970s.

Social scientists attribute the bulk of this rise to changes in sentencing policies and politics, rather than changes in the underlying rate of crime, which has fallen dramatically over much of the mass incarceration era. Violent crime rates experienced growth, fluctuation, and substantial decline over the past 50 years, a very different pattern than incarceration (especially after 1990). So while crime clearly plays some part in the story, most punishment scholars agree that social policy changes, such as the war on drugs, mandatory minimum sentences, and other "get tough" measures, are most responsible for the growth.

Beyond incarceration, other forms of criminal punishment have also shot up in recent years. As the next graph

U.S. Incarceration & Violent Crime Rates

Sources: BJS, State and Federal Prisoners, 1925-1985; BJS trends since 1980 (http://bjs.ojp.usdoj.gov/content/glance/tables/incrttab.cfm); Uniform Crime Rates (http://www.ucrdatatool.gov/)

shows, the vast majority of people who are under supervision by the criminal justice system are not in prison or jail at all. Instead, they are living in their communities while supervised on parole (a conditional early release from prison) or probation (a sentence in place of jail or prison time). All of these populations have grown, rising from less than two million people under correctional supervision in 1980 to about seven million in 2011.

In addition to these increases in punishment rates, the likelihood of *arrest* has also risen over time. In a 2012 *Pediat-*

U.S. Correctional Populations

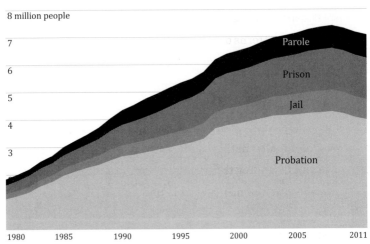

Sources: Bureau of Justice Statistics, Annual Probation Survey, Annual Parole Survey, Annual Survey of Jails, Census of Jail Inmates, and National Prisoner Statistics Program, 2000-2011.

rics article, Robert Brame and his colleagues estimate that the likelihood of arrest for Americans under 23 has grown from less than one in four in the 1960s to one in three by the 2000s.

space

Social facts are located in space as well as time, as the "Chicago School" of sociology has demonstrated for almost a century. With today's tools for collecting and analyzing geographic data, it has become much easier to see exactly how spatial context matters for a host of social problems. Criminologists and police departments use crime mapping and "hot spot" analysis, for example, to identify, understand, and address patterns of crime in urban areas.

Rates of punishment vary greatly by geographic location, and there are *radical* differences in imprisonment rates across nations and states. The map on the following page is a cartogram, which distorts the shape and size of land area based on an alternative statistic—in this case, incarceration rates. Changing the familiar dimensions helps us visualize where punishment is unusually high and low, since the nations appear as bloated or emaciated on the incarceration-adjusted cartogram.

The legend at the bottom shows that, in 2011, the United States was the only nation with a combined rate of prison and jail incarceration of over 600 per 100,000. Thus, the United States, with the world's highest total rate of incarceration (743 per 100,000, including jail inmates), is greatly inflated on the cartogram. Despite the fact that prison populations have grown worldwide, the United States has outpaced every other country, exceeding the incarceration levels of other democratic nations by five to seven times. Our closest competitors in 2011 were Rwanda (595) and Russia (568).

As compared to a more typical map, the cartogram brings more punitive nations into bold relief. It also dramatically downsizes nations with incarceration rates below 150 per 100,000 people, such as Canada and much of Europe and

World Rates of Incarceration, 2011

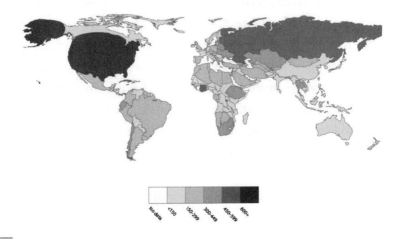

No data   <150   150-299   300-449   450-599   600+

Africa. Other nations that are large in land area but lower in incarceration rates, such as China and India, are also notably diminished in size.

The next set of maps shows how rates of punishment vary almost as dramatically *within* the United States as across the globe. In the cartogram on page 50, the percentage of the adult population in prison in 2010 ranged from less than .25% in Maine and Minnesota to over 1% in Alaska and Louisiana. The lion's share of these differences can be attributed to policy choices about which types of crimes trigger which types of sentences; states that impose life sentences after "three strikes," for example, tend to have higher incarceration rates. These policies are influenced by differences in crime rates, political culture, economics, and demographics. For example, sociologists David Greenberg and Valerie West traced state incarceration growth to rates of violent crime and conservative political cultures.

This state-level imprisonment variation is amplified and altered when depicted by race. The next cartogram on page 51 displays the percentage of adult African Americans who were imprisoned in each state in 2010. Overall, this map is more darkly shaded than the map for total incarceration, since most states incarcerate at least 2% of their African American residents. In contrast to the overall map, predominantly white states such as Iowa, Wisconsin, and Vermont appear bloated,

Percent of U.S. Adults in Prison by State, 2010

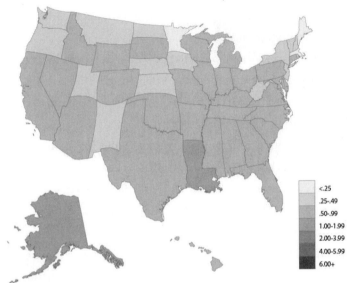

	<.25
	.25-.49
	.50-.99
	1.00-1.99
	2.00-3.99
	4.00-5.99
	6.00+

with each locking up more than 4% of African American adults. These high rates are not the simple result of African Americans committing more crime. There are also race differences in the responses of the criminal justice system, especially in situations where its workers have great discretion. For example, research by criminologist Jeffrey Fagan and colleagues suggests that police officers are more likely to stop and to arrest African Americans for low-level drug crimes.

Hispanic incarceration is trickier to plot because states have not consistently collected information on Hispanic

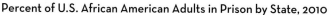

Percent of U.S. African American Adults in Prison by State, 2010

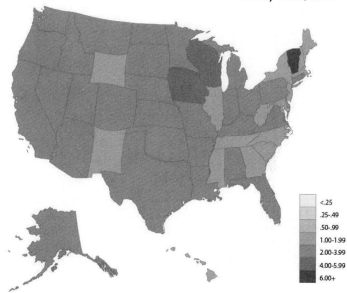

	<.25
	.25-.49
	.50-.99
	1.00-1.99
	2.00-3.99
	4.00-5.99
	6.00+

ethnicity, often confounding it with racial categories. But the simple map on the next page shows that the percentage of adults of Hispanic origin also varies significantly by state, with a strong geographic pattern of higher rates in the western half of the country.

Somewhat different patterns emerge when we map percentages of the adult population under correctional supervision for felony-level crimes, regardless of whether they are behind bars or in the community. States like Georgia and

Percent of U.S. Hispanic Adults in Prison, 2010

	<.25
	.25-.49
	.50-.99
	1.00-1.99
	2.00-3.99
	4.00-5.99
	6.00+

Minnesota have high rates of probation supervision, so they appear more swollen in page 53's cartogram than in the incarceration cartograms.

As with incarceration, there are big racial differences in correctional supervision. The cartogram on page 54 shows the percentage of adult African Americans under correctional control for felonies in each state in 2010. More than 4% of adult African Americans were under supervision for felony convictions in at least 16 states. Compared to the previous cartogram of the overall population, states such as California, Iowa, Oregon, and Wisconsin are darker and enlarged,

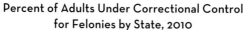

Percent of Adults Under Correctional Control
for Felonies by State, 2010

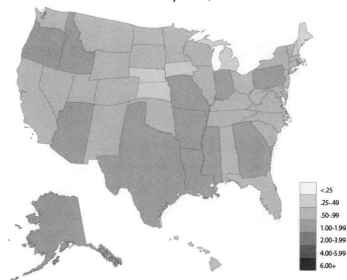

<.25
.25-.49
.50-.99
1.00-1.99
2.00-3.99
4.00-5.99
6.00+

revealing especially high rates of African American correctional supervision. A similar map of Hispanic correctional supervision would show particularly high rates in the southwest and upper plains states.

Visualizing punishment across the states shows that there is no single picture of punishment in the United States. States make diverse policy and sentencing choices, each of which affects the scale and composition of their correctional populations. While a national picture is useful for comparing countries and displaying trends over time, the

Percent of Adult African Americans Under Correctional Control for Felonies by State, 2010

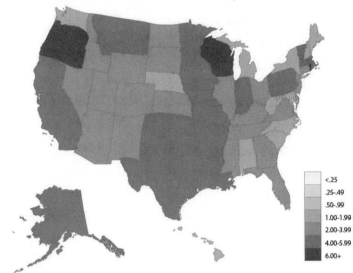

| <.25 |
| .25-.49 |
| .50-.99 |
| 1.00-1.99 |
| 2.00-3.99 |
| 4.00-5.99 |
| 6.00+ |

most important decisions about who is punished and how punishment is carried out are often made at the state or local level.

social concentration

The maps we've shown so far illustrate the astonishing concentration of punishment by race in the United States, especially among African Americans. But when race is combined with other demographic factors, the social concentration of punishment is even more pronounced. The intersection of race, social class, and incarceration is especially powerful.

Sociologist Bruce Western and his colleagues have estimated that, for recent cohorts of African American men with no high school degree, the lifetime likelihood of going to prison is roughly 60%—about five times higher than the corresponding rate for white high school dropouts. Spending time in prison has become a statistically normative life experience for young African American men with low education. The chart on the next page illustrates these disparities, showing that one third of young African American male dropouts were incarcerated in 2000, compared with about 6% of whites and Hispanics. According to Western's analysis, twice as many African American men born in the late 1960s had prison records as had college degrees by 1999.

Punishment is also socially concentrated in low-income, urban areas. Criminologist Todd Clear reports that more than 18% of male residents in some Cleveland and Baltimore neighborhoods are incarcerated and one in five adult men in Washington, D.C., are behind bars on any given day. Similarly, over half of all prisoners released in the states of Illinois and Maryland return to the cities of Chicago and Baltimore, respectively. According to Jeremy Travis, president of John Jay College of Criminal Justice, more than a third of these returning prisoners are concentrated in just a

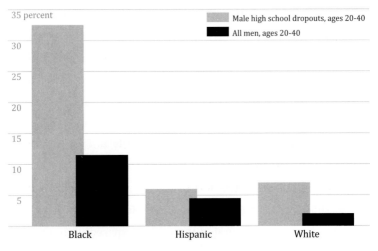

Male Incarceration Rate in 2000 by Race, Ethnicity, and Education

Source: Western, Bruce. 2006. *Punishment and Inequality in America*. New York: Russell Sage. P. 19.

handful of neighborhoods. Eric Cadora and colleagues at the Justice Mapping Center have gone further to show that correctional control varies not just by neighborhood but by city block. Some states spend upward of a million dollars each year incarcerating the residents of just one city block. As residents of these "million-dollar blocks" move in and out of prison, the communities lose valuable social and human capital, a process Clear and others describe as "reentry cycling."

The map of New York state and New York City (inset) on page 57 shows how rates of prison release vary at the county and zip-code level. Counties with urban centers such as

Albany, Syracuse, and New York appear darker on the map, indicating higher rates of prison releases. In New York City, these releases are clearly more concentrated in low-income neighborhoods and those populated by persons of color, including Harlem, the South Bronx, Bedford-Stuyvesant in Brooklyn, and Jamaica in Queens.

Each of these visualizations reminds us that punishment is not randomly distributed across the population, but is instead highly concentrated among certain subpopulations and locations. As David Garland puts it, mass incarceration in the United States is not simply defined by the imprisonment

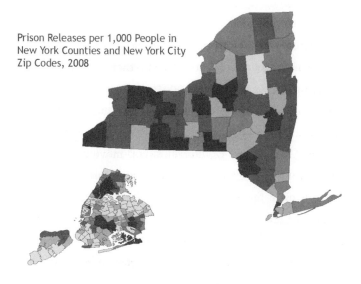

Prison Releases per 1,000 People in
New York Counties and New York City
Zip Codes, 2008

of large numbers of people but by the "systematic imprisonment of whole groups of the population."

punishment effects

The social costs of the U.S. policy experiment with mass imprisonment are widespread and staggering, especially for the most disadvantaged segments of the population. Recent evidence from sociologist Becky Pettit suggests that previously touted gains for young African American men, such as higher voter turnout and lower high school dropout rates, diminish (and, in some cases, disappear completely) once the figures are adjusted to include incarcerated persons.

Incarceration deepens existing inequalities and even creates new inequalities on multiple dimensions, including the labor market, family, and political participation. Stigma gained by virtue of contact with the criminal justice system lasts well beyond the completion of sentence, especially for African Americans. Collateral sanctions, such as exclusions from employment, voting, and public assistance, make it even more challenging for people with criminal records to gain a foothold in society. As a result, many criminologists view both prisons and their collateral consequences as *criminogenic*—ultimately contributing to *more* crime rather than less as people cycle in and out of the system with little access to the economic, social, and political resources that would help them "make good" on the outside.

States are pursuing radically different alternatives to many collateral sanctions. This variation serves as a good illustration of the dramatic range of options at a state's (or a nation's) disposal. For example, a remarkable 5.85 million Americans are forbidden to vote because of "felon disenfranchisement," laws restricting voting rights for those convicted of felony-level crimes. Of this total, which represents about 2.5% of the U.S. voting-age population, over two million are African Americans. But as the cartogram on page 60 shows, these laws vary significantly by state. More than 7% of the adult population is disenfranchised in states like Alabama, Florida, Kentucky, Mississippi, Tennessee, and Virginia where people lose their voting rights for life, but *none* of the population is disenfranchised in Maine and Vermont, where even current prisoners retain the franchise.

Public opinion research shows that most Americans favor voting rights for probationers and parolees, as well as for former felons who have completed their sentences. If state laws were changed to reflect these principles, voting rights would be restored to well over four million people—and the cartogram would more closely resemble a standard U.S. map.

Percent of the Adult Population Disenfranchised Due to Felony Conviction by State, 2010

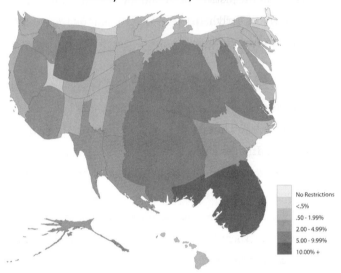

No Restrictions
<.5%
.50 - 1.99%
2.00 - 4.99%
5.00 - 9.99%
10.00% +

alternative visions

Given the scope and magnitude of America's experiment with mass incarceration, it will be some time before social scientists chase down all of its effects. Most societies seem to require some degree of incarceration to preserve public safety, but *mass* imprisonment implies a degree of excess punishment beyond what's required to control crime—leaving observers searching for alternatives. How crime is punished is a social policy choice, and other visions of punishment are possible, given the political will to change. Such alternative visions might include redirection of low-level offenses away from the criminal justice system, fewer long prison sentences, judicious use of early release, a general shift from prison to community corrections, a budget transfer from corrections to law enforcement and crime prevention, and a reduction in the scope and number of collateral sanctions.

If we are to see our way toward a new vision of crime and its control in the United States, we must first see punishment as it is. Images are an important means for telling the story of racialized mass incarceration—its rapid growth over time, its variation across space, and its concentration within particular populations. Ideally, such visualizations will not only help us to grasp the state of punishment but to begin to envision how it might be changed.

RECOMMENDED READING

Todd Clear. 2007. *Imprisoning Communities: How Mass Incarceration Makes Disadvantaged Neighborhoods Worse*, New York: Oxford University Press. An authoritative analysis of punishment and urban communities.

David Garland. 2001. *The Culture of Control: Crime and Social Order in Contemporary Society*, Chicago: University of Chicago Press. Shows how criminal justice policies of mass incarceration exemplify the basic problems of governance in the modern world.

David F. Greenberg and Valerie West. 2001. "State Prison Populations and Their Growth, 1971–1991," *Criminology* 39:615–654. A careful quantitative study of the factors driving changes in state imprisonment rates.

Becky Pettit. 2012. *Invisible Men: Mass Incarceration and the Myth of Black Progress*, New York: Russell Sage. A cogent analysis of how mass incarceration conceals racial inequalities in education, employment, and politics.

Bruce Western. 2006. *Punishment and Inequality in America*, New York: Russell Sage. Powerfully documents the growth and social costs of incarceration for individuals and communities.

cultural contexts

why punishment
is purple

JOSHUA PAGE

On December 15, 2010, a group of conservative politicians and activists officially launched the Right on Crime initiative, creating a stir among criminal justice reporters, reformers, and scholars. Luminaries of the right—including antitax crusader Grover Norquist, notoriously "tough on crime" former Speaker of the House New Gingrich, and former "Drug Czar," radio host, and champion of the war on crime William Bennett—signed a pledge to reform criminal justice. Among other things, the conservatives called for limiting "overcriminalization," expanding drug courts, decreasing mandatory minimum sentences for nonviolent offenders, and increasing alternatives to imprisonment.

Right on Crime argued that runaway penal expansion violated the conservative principles of small government, fiscal responsibility, and individual liberty. That the likes of Gingrich and Bennett—the same men who had previously mocked or ignored critics of the wars on drugs and crime—recognized the need for reform surprised and pleased progressive activists and organizations. Conservative Republicans advocating penal change? Maybe the tide was turning.

While advocates applauded the Right on Crime initiative, they wrung their hands at the Obama administration's actions concerning penal policy—especially drug policy. When Barack Obama assumed the presidency, progressives hoped he'd draw attention to the detrimental effects of mass imprisonment on public coffers, social services, and low-income, minority individuals and communities. They thought Obama would support changes in sentencing policy and law enforcement practices and push for federal spending for prisoner reentry. Instead, the administration has continued—and, in some respects, intensified—the war on drugs and other penal policies. Obama's lackluster approach to crime and punishment issues has disappointed reformers.

These opposing feelings—excitement about Right on Crime and displeasure with Obama's actions—are due largely to a belief that criminal justice is a red and blue issue. That is, Republicans favor harsh penal sanctions and oppose rehabilitation, while Democrats support less punitive penalties and more rehabilitation and treatment. Right on Crime and Obama's positions seem to defy common sense about the politics of punishment.

A strong line of social science research shows that this "common sense" is wrong. Crime politics do not fit neatly within a red versus blue framework. Although it is true that Republicans ignited the "law and order" movement in the 1960s, Democrats have supported—and, at times, initiated—incredibly punitive policies for over three decades. Further, Republican lawmakers and conservative states have initiated some of the most promising criminal justice reforms in recent years. Belying typical party labels, punishment today is a curious shade of purple.

forging a bipartisan consensus

Throughout the 1960s and '70s, Republicans earned the label "tough on crime." From Barry Goldwater to Richard Nixon and Ronald Reagan, Republicans used crime and punishment to broaden their base and win elections. As part of the "Southern Strategy," Republicans' effort to break up the New Deal Coalition and pull white voters from the Democratic Party, right wing politicians lashed out at "street criminals" and "welfare queens"—code for poor, urban minorities. Promising an era of law and order, Republicans appealed to white voters who felt uneasy as social movements shook the racial, gender, and sexual orders; the economy underwent major restructuring and high crime became a social fact. As demonstrated by sociologist Katherine Beckett, though, Republicans didn't make criminal justice a central political issue in response to public pressure; voters did not list fear of crime as a top concern until after politicians began insisting street crime was public enemy number one. Republicans effectively created public pressure around crime.

Into the 1980s, Republicans continued to use crime as a wedge. Renowned legal scholar John Hagan documents in his recent book, *Who Are the Criminals?* that it didn't take long for Democrats to realize the danger of pushing against the punitive tide. The only realistic political option was to join forces, pumping resources into law enforcement and pushing for mandatory punishment of street crimes. In one naked attempt to neutralize Republicans' success with the crime issue, Democratic Speaker of the House Tip O'Neill took advantage of a moral panic about crack cocaine to enact the Anti-Drug Abuse Act of 1986, including its infamous 100 to 1 rule that mandated five years in prison for possession of five grams of crack cocaine or *five hundred* grams of powder cocaine. Because crack was concentrated in low-income African American communities while cocaine was associated with the white middle and upper class, critics charged the 100 to 1 rule was clear evidence that the war on drugs was really a war on poor blacks.

Nationally, Democrats' efforts to undermine Republicans' advantage on the crime issue peaked during Bill Clinton's campaign and presidency. Clinton was determined not to meet the same fate as Michael Dukakis, who had been handicapped by claims that he was soft on crime in the '88 presidential election. While Dukakis had been governor of Massachusetts, convicted murderer Willie Horton participated in a weekend furlough program Dukakis supported in the name of rehabilitation. During his furlough, Horton raped a woman and brutally beat her fiancé. Dukakis's presidential opponent, George H. W. Bush, seized on this, repeatedly blaming Dukakis for Horton's release and crimes and using famous ads to tie the two in the public consciousness. The message was clear: if elected, Dukakis would let scary black men like Horton roam free to rape and murder "law-abiding" individuals (read: middle-class whites). Soon, few doubted Bush would win the election.

In Bill Clinton's presidential campaign, a key moment occurred on January 24, 1992. Then governor of Arkansas, Clinton returned home to oversee the execution of a severely brain-damaged black man, Ricky Ray Rector, who had killed a white police officer. Along with denying Rector clemency, the candidate's highly publicized jaunt off the campaign trail demonstrated that he, unlike Dukakis, was unquestionably pro-death penalty (i.e., tough on crime) and pro-law enforcement. *Time* magazine quoted Clinton: "I can be nicked a lot, but no one can say I'm soft on crime." Pregnant with racial symbolism, Clinton indicated that he would strike down—rather than furlough or otherwise try to rehabilitate—criminals like Rector and Horton; he'd stand up for (white) victims and law-abiding citizens. The boost Clinton gained from the Rector execution is unclear. However, less than a month later, he finished a strong second in the New Hampshire primary, resuscitating a presidential quest that'd been weakened by allegations of marital infidelity and draft dodging.

After Clinton moved into the White House, he continued to show he was tough on lawbreakers and further narrowed the divide between Democrats and Republicans on crime issues. In September 1994, Clinton proudly signed the most expansive crime bill in history. Arguably the president's crowning achievement, the bipartisan legislation contained sentencing provisions—including a federal Three Strikes law—targeting repeat offenders, juveniles as young as 13, sex offenders, and drug criminals. The bill expanded the death penalty; incentivized states to implement "truth-in-sentencing" laws, which mandate convicts serve at least 85% of their sentences; and increased the size and capacity of the penal system with funding for 100,000 new police officers, $9.7 billion for prisons, and $2.6 billion for law enforcement agencies including the Federal Bureau of Investigation, Drug

Enforcement Administration, Immigration and Naturalization Service, and the U.S. Attorneys' Office. The legislation also denied Pell Grants, the main source of funding for college behind bars, to prisoners, thereby hardening the conditions of confinement and eliminating a well-established means for decreasing recidivism and aiding prison management.

The crime bill did include several preventative and rehabilitative provisions that provided money for programs for at-risk youth, prison-based drug treatment, drug courts, and domestic violence prevention. To the chagrin of the gun lobby, it banned some types of assault rifles and stiffened firearm licensing and purchasing regulations.

In all, the 1994 bill exemplified the "new Democrat" approach to crime issues—be as punitive as Republicans while maintaining an emphasis on prevention and, to a lesser extent, rehabilitation. In employing this triangulated strategy, Democrats sought to insulate themselves from "soft on crime" accusations while also appeasing constituencies that opposed laws like Three Strikes and supported crime prevention and offender treatment. It was a precarious position.

golden opportunities

The purpling of punishment occurred in several key states but, as I document in my book, *The Toughest Beat,* nowhere was this more evident than in California, often a trailblazer in penal matters. As governor, Ronald Reagan masterfully used "law and order" to advance his agenda and career. Reagan's successor, Democrat Jerry Brown, took office in 1975 as the tough-on-crime fury spread and intensified—he signified a gradual rightward movement of the state's Democratic leaders.

Criticized for opposing the death penalty and appointing liberal judges to California's Supreme Court, in 1976 Brown signed the state's determinate sentencing law, shifting sentencing power from judges and parole boards to prosecutors and legislators, who quickly instituted long mandatory prison terms for countless crimes. The law also redefined the official mission of imprisonment from rehabilitation to punishment. Geographer Ruth Wilson Gilmore, in her political-economic analysis of California's prison construction boom, shows that the Brown administration ignited the explosion.

By the '90s, California's Democratic leadership was practically indistinguishable from Republicans on issues of crime and punishment. This blurring was evident in the events leading up to the passage of the state's Three Strikes law in 1994. The brainchild of a father of a murdered child and conservative activists, the Repeat Offender law was far more radical than the Three Strikes law implemented earlier in Washington state. Its predecessor targeted only offenders convicted of three very serious crimes, but the California law called for sentences of 25-to-life for those convicted of two serious crimes and any felony—even low-level crimes would trigger a life sentence.

Democrats initially balked, claiming Three Strikes would affect too many and further crowd the state's brimming prisons. But as the prospects of Three Strikes remained unclear, a recently paroled repeat offender kidnapped, raped, and murdered a white girl in the sleepy California town of Petaluma. A media-driven moral panic about "career criminals" sprang up, and high-profile Democrats lined up behind a ballot initiative to implement the nation's most punitive Three Strikes law. After it passed, powerful Democrats in the executive and legislative branches worked to protect the measure from reform or elimination.

Democratic support for Three Strikes quickly spread beyond California. The graphic on page 74 shows, of all of the states with Three Strikes, more had Democratic than Republican governors when the law was passed. Similarly, more of the states' legislatures were under Democratic control. Three Strikes is a purple phenomenon.

In promoting Three Strikes across the country, Democrats tried to neutralize the Republican advantage on punishment and connect with voters inundated with sensational accounts of lawbreaking. By supporting the law, Democrats

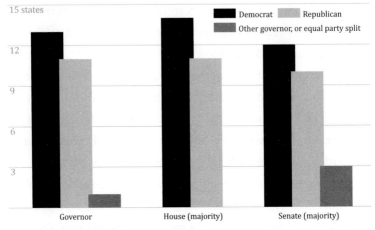

Political Environment of States at Passage of Three Strikes Legislation

15 states

■ Democrat ▨ Republican
▨ Other governor, or equal party split

12

9

6

3

Governor   House (majority)   Senate (majority)

Sources:
    University of Kentucky Center for Poverty Research, State-Level Data on Economic, Political, and Transfer-Program Information for 1980-2010
    James Austin, John Clark, Patricia Hardyman, and Alan Henry, Three Strikes and You're Out: The Implementation and Impacts of Strike Laws, (National Institute of Justice, 1999)

endorsed the conservative view of crime and punishment—
Three Strikes, for example, affirms the idea that repeat
offenders are irredeemable "others" who must be eliminated
("struck out"), eschewing rehabilitation for incapacitation
and vengeance. Likewise, mandatory minimums disre-
gard individual circumstances and social context, defining
offenders solely by their crimes. Through measures like this,
the punitive turn in American criminal justice has been
facilitated by Democrats and Republicans alike.

Several years after California instituted the nation's
most stringent Three Strikes law, Gray Davis completed

the process. Whereas Brown toughened up on crime in the course of his gubernatorial term, Davis promised to crack down on lawbreakers from the outset. In addition to protecting himself from "weak on crime" charges and appealing to white voters, Davis had a third motivation for establishing the "prosecutor in chief" persona (a term criminologist Jonathan Simon uses for politicians who act as if their main job is to combat crime and take on issues like educational underachievement as if they were crimes): Davis hoped to secure finances and endorsements from authoritative interest groups, especially the state's powerful prison officers' union and punitive-oriented crime victims' groups.

Indeed, in his tightly contested 1998 gubernatorial race against Republican state attorney general Dan Lungren, the prison officers' union spent more than $2 million on television commercials that touted Davis's tough stances on crime. In office, Davis continued to benefit from his relationship with the officers' union and victims' groups; the labor group spent more than $3 million on his behalf and the victims' organizations routinely used their moral authority to validate Davis's tough-on-crime bona fides.

As shown so clearly in California, Democratic leaders throughout the United States took positions previously associated with Republicans not just to defend against claims that they were soft on crime. Like their Republican colleagues, they also lurched rightward to gain votes (especially from working- and middle-class whites) and favors (from influential interest groups). Because of the many political benefits and limited risks, politicians like Davis couldn't resist assuming the role of prosecutor in chief.

In the 1990s, this is to say, high-ranking Democrats fully realized the opportunities of crime politics Republicans had understood at least since the late 1960s. Although leading Democrats joined Republicans in passing ultra-tough penal measures, it's important to note that many rank-and-file Democrats (especially those from solidly blue and predominantly minority communities) resisted pressures to veer right, continuing to advocate for prevention, rehabilitation, and reasonable sentencing laws. Far more variation and contestation over penal matters remained within the Democratic than the Republican party, which has been generally unified on crime issues. Therefore, in an excellent review essay, "On the Politics of Imprisonments," Aubrey Jackson and David Jacobs describe strong, independent relationships between Republican political strength and indicators of punitiveness: imprisonment rates, financing for prison expansion, and capital punishment (both in terms of legality and quantity of executions). Their findings suggest that, although high-profile "new Democrats" like Bill Clinton and Gray Davis got caught up in the punitive tide, other Democrats have challenged the purpling of punishment. If Democrats were unified in being tough on crime, Democratic political strength also would be positively related to punitiveness.

purple haze

Over the last several decades, bipartisan agreement has developed in crime politics, propelling distinctly punitive penal priorities, policies, and practices. This crime consensus is key to understanding the incredible growth of American imprisonment—as well as its focus on street crime and disproportionate effects on low-income blacks and Latinos. As is now known beyond academic and reform circles, the United States, with over 1.6 million people in state and federal prisons, has the world's highest incarceration rate. Though serious crime has declined steadily since the early 1990s, we are only now seeing decreases in state prison populations. The federal prison population continues to grow.

Moreover, the recent drops in state prison numbers are the result of reforms—mostly changes to parole—enacted primarily because of budget crises and, in some cases, demands from the federal courts to ease crowding. Some of the most meaningful policy changes have been implemented in conservative states such as Arkansas, Kentucky, Nebraska, and Texas.

Like the Right on Crime initiative, red-state penal reform has garnered significant attention from the media and liberal advocacy organizations—it is simply counterintuitive given the Right's rigid commitment to "law and order." But these unexpected developments are not just the result of fiscal and judicial pressures; they're also due to Democratic success in neutralizing crime as an effective wedge issue. Increasingly, Republicans see little political advantage in being tougher than thou.

Finally, while significant in recent history, state reforms have been quite modest—the reduction of New York's notoriously harsh Rockefeller drug laws is one obvious exception. Truly reducing the size and costs (both fiscal and human) of the penal system would require major changes to sentencing laws, including those dealing with serious and violent offenders. Democrats and Republicans remain unlikely to promote the overhauls capable of drawing down (and keeping down) the correctional population.

They are reluctant to take bold action because of the fear of crime politics. The ghost of Willie Horton haunts politicians, red and blue. From a crude political standpoint, there is simply too much to lose and too little to win to go out on a limb here. So, ironically, for high-profile Democrats to embrace top-to-bottom penal transformation, Republicans may have to take the lead. Since Republicans remain ideologically opposed to reducing prison terms for everyone except low-level drug offenders, though, it's doubtful they'll embrace the large-scale reforms needed to shrink the penal system.

Taken together, it appears that the twenty-first century's politics of punishment is becoming a new shade of purple, with lawmakers from both parties supporting just enough change to bring down costs and ease prison overcrowding. The slight variation in hue, however, will not be enough to end mass imprisonment.

RECOMMENDED READING

Katherine Beckett. 1999. *Making Crime Pay: Law and Order in Contemporary American Politics*, New York: Oxford University Press. Shows that the politics of law and order was a Republican strategy to lure white voters away from the Democratic Party.

Marie Gottschalk. 2006. *The Prison and the Gallows: The Politics of Mass Incarceration in America*, Cambridge, UK: Cambridge University Press. Explains how the political and institutional infrastructure for mass incarceration developed well before the 1960s.

John Hagan. 2010. *Who Are the Criminals? The Politics of Crime Policy from the Age of Roosevelt to the Age of Reagan*, Princeton, NJ: Princeton University Press. Provides clear examples of Democrats' efforts to neutralize Republicans' advantage in the area of crime and punishment, showing how both parties de-emphasized penalties for corporate crime while cracking down on street crime.

Aubrey Jackson and David Jacobs. 2010. "On the Politics of Imprisonments: A Review of Systematic Findings," *Annual Review of Law and Social Science* 6: 129–149. Summarizes studies on the relationship between politics and incarceration, and identifies differences in political and legal institutions that help explain why America's imprisonment rate is so high.

Jonathan Simon. 2007. *Governing through Crime: How the War on Crime Transformed American Democracy and Created a Culture of Fear,* New York: Oxford University Press. Shows that politicians in the second half of the twentieth century used crime to frame a wide range of social issues and exert authority. It also documents how this framework influenced institutions of civil society (like schools) in the 1980s.

6

the color purple

JONATHAN SIMON

n the previous chapter, "Why Punishment Is Purple,"
Joshua Page astutely updates the political sociology of mass
incarceration. The story of conservative/Republican success in using crime as a wedge issue was told first by political
observers and then more rigorously by sociologists and
criminologists. Republicans saw fear of violent crime and,
frankly, any kind of crime they associated with declining
property values as an emerging issue for white, blue-collar
Democrats who were running out of benefits they could get
from a New Deal-type state and whose anxieties about race
were increasingly out of bounds in the Democratic Party.
After Bill Clinton, however, Republicans lost their advantage. Today, some Republicans are outdistancing Democrats
in offering innovative alternatives to the penal state. Page
turns to California to demonstrate the political dynamics in
more detail.

Page believes that the latest news in this area is not likely to
mark a new political competition to bring down imprisonment

rates and dismantle the institutional logics of crime fear as citizenship. Instead, politicians will tinker in the shadow of Willie Horton, afraid to do more than experiment with decarcerating the shallow end of the felony pool. Purple America, whether governed by Obama or Romney, is likely to remain a highly incarcerated America.

There is little I can disagree with in this overall depressing picture. The Republican edge on crime was, in my view, never all that solid. Robert Kennedy was one of the first really effective dealers in the new politics of crime, and he managed to blend neo-welfarist strategies (for juveniles) with a preparedness to back a tough police response to urban crime and violence. While the bullets that brought him down prevented us from thinking of RFK as the "war on crime" president he might have been instead of Nixon, it was not, I think, a lack of understanding that prevented Democrats from taking on crime as a close study of their policy ideas in the period would show. Instead, the Democrats were hampered by truly mixed reactions to the prospects of enlarging and empowering urban police forces at a time when many liberal Democrats, black and white, feared the police as much or more than crime (this was post-1968).

In contrast, while Republicans had no fear of the police, neither did they have a strong desire to invest in an urban police force. Indeed, as the late Bill Stuntz emphasizes in his great, posthumously published *The Collapse of the American Criminal Justice* and as my colleague Justin McCrary has shown in his work, police were largely ignored after 1980 in favor of mass incarceration, a strategy that held strong appeals for white suburban homeowners and little that Democrats or liberals found inherently troubling.

Perhaps like Shug in *The Color Purple*, I'm just at a stage of life where I'm more ready to seek out hope. I do think some of the underlying cultural politics that made mass incarceration such an appealing tool have been eroded. One is "white flight." So long as white families saw their future in ever more distant satellite suburbs with exclusionary zoning and other segregation strategies, they looked to mass incarceration to express their anxieties about urban crime and showed little interest in supporting urban policing. But, as research by Reynolds Farley and his colleagues suggests (see "The Waning of American Apartheid," *Contexts*, Summer 2011), whites today are far less ready to move away from minority populations than they were in the '80s. The energy crisis and a backlash against suburban automobility are also fueling an urban comeback, and its fate is surely tied up with the waning of apartheid and, in turn, with fear of crime. But while fear or its shadow will remain a powerful driver, both have made a police versus prison strategy more plausible than it has been in a couple of generations. Of course, that assumes we can convince police to stop acting in racist and counterproductive ways to degrade young men of color and pull them into the prison system.

Another reason for optimism is that the moral legitimacy of mass incarceration is more vulnerable than it has been in decades. Despite tags like "the new Jim Crow," mass incarceration retains its legitimacy for many Americans, white and nonwhite, who see it as a way to hold "dangerous men, securely, in humane conditions" (as the terms of an important Supreme Court opinion, *Farmer v. Brennan,* put it). However, the truth about American prisons, as revealed to the nation by Justice Kennedy's majority opinion in the California prison health-care crisis case *Brown v. Plata* last year, is that they increasingly hold a chronically ill and aging population—more at risk than posing a risk—and that they are neither securely nor humanely held. All of this has the power to erode mass imprisonment's legitimacy.

This "Abu Ghraib moment" is already affecting the penal imaginary of the elite (just look at the number of stories on the qualitative dimension of incarceration that have come out since *Brown*). This isn't the same as reaching the general public, but it is a hopeful sign. The crime-fear wave of the '60s circulated first among journalists, lawyers, and other elites (who saw a largely fictional crime wave in the 1950s), then spread to the wider public. The humanitarian response to mass incarceration, so evident in Justice Kennedy's mention of torture and emphatic embrace of dignity as the animating meaning of the Eighth Amendment, may also spread from the consciousness of legal elites to a broader audience.

repercussions of incarceration on close relationships

MEGAN COMFORT

When an arrest is made, all eyes are on the person in handcuffs. At a trial, the jury focuses intently upon the defendant. And when the prison door slams shut, we envision the solitary individual "doing time" far from the outside world. The *outlaw*, the *offender*: even the words commonly used to describe people who are arrested, sentenced, and incarcerated suggest loners, isolated beings whose only interactions involve other lawbreakers, crime victims, and police and correctional officers.

And yet, as social scientists turn their gaze to the surrounding streets, residences, courthouse hallways, and correctional visiting rooms, we expand our view of who is affected by the criminal justice system. We are alerted to children hiding in closets during a parent's arrest or coming home from school to an empty apartment. They may eventually wind up in the custody of grandparents, in the child welfare system, or, worse still, in juvenile custody. We become aware of mothers and fathers whose doors are broken down in the dead of the night and who are held at gunpoint in their bedclothes as the police search for their fugitive sons or daughters. We realize that, like everyone, people who are suspected or convicted of breaking the law have families, friends, and neighbors who experience profound psychological, social, economic, and health consequences when they have an outstanding warrant, get sent to jail, or come home from prison with a felony record. Arresting, sentencing, and incarcerating one person reverberates through familial and social networks. Like the cue ball breaking the rack in billiards, the punishment of one person sends many others spinning off in multiple directions.

ripple effects

In the United States, the need to establish what sociologist Robert Sampson calls a "social ledger of incarceration's effects"—an assessment of its impacts on personal and family relations and neighborhood stability—has become urgent. The number of people coming into contact with the criminal justice system has ballooned. According to the Bureau of

Justice Statistics (BJS), there were roughly 380,000 people behind bars in the United States in the mid-1970s, and some of the nation's most distinguished criminologists predicted that prisons were on their way to extinction. Instead, there now are over 2.2 million people in jail or prison on any given day, and millions more cycle through correctional facilities each year. Given the available data, we cannot know precisely how many family members, social intimates, and neighbors are affected by these events, but we can begin to make an educated guess. As one example, BJS statisticians Lauren Glaze and Laura Maruschak report that just over half of the nation's prisoners reported that they were parents to an estimated 1.7 million minor children in 2007; that would mean 2.3% of the U.S. population under age 18 had a parent in state or federal prison. (Keep in mind, these numbers do not include the children of people who were in local jails; many more people go to jail than to prison because prisons generally are reserved for convicts serving longer sentences for more serious crimes, while jails hold anyone awaiting judicial disposition and those convicted of minor offenses.)

Criminal justice involvement is extremely unevenly distributed across the population. Indeed, sociologist Loïc Wacquant argues that rather than "mass incarceration," which implies a generalized experience concerning broad segments of the population (as with mass media or mass transit), the

U.S. penal state has created a phenomenon of "hyperincarceration" by targeting policing and punishment policies "first by class, second by race, and third by place." In other words, the people who are most likely to wind up under arrest, facing a prosecutor, and sitting behind bars are overwhelmingly those who are extremely poor (two thirds of jail inmates come from a household living under one half of the official poverty line), African American, and reside in neighborhoods of concentrated disadvantage and dysfunctional public institutions. By extension, the people who are most likely to experience a family member's incarceration are *also* disproportionately impoverished African Americans. Sociologist Christopher Wildeman calculated that black children born in 1990 had a 25.1% risk of having their father imprisoned by the time they were 14 years old, compared with a 3.6% risk for white children born in the same year. Tellingly, the Fragile Families and Child Wellbeing Study and other poverty research not focused on incarceration per se has provided critical data about the reach and scope of people affected by the criminal justice system through their connection to arrestees and inmates. Indeed, incarceration has become so prevalent among the nation's poor that it influences every institution and status, from employment and education to housing, public health, and family formation.

"secondary prisonization"

My interest in what I call the "repercussive effects" of incarceration began when I worked at the San Quentin State Prison visiting center in the late 1990s. San Quentin is located in northern California, directly across the bay from San Francisco, and it's the oldest prison in the state. California law mandates that each prison has a center to assist visitors, a primary function of which is to provide clothing for people to borrow if they arrive dressed in garments that are prohibited by the correctional facility. These items include anything that prisoners or prison officers wear, such as blue jeans, white T-shirts, button-up chambray shirts, and the colors khaki, bright yellow, and army green. Visitors must pass through a metal detector before being allowed into the prison. (For the dozen years I spent at San Quentin, the machine was calibrated so sensitively that the underwire in a bra would set off the alarm and trigger denial of entry.)

My early days at the visiting center were regularly punctuated by people—mainly wives and girlfriends, mothers and sisters, often with young children—showing up at our doorstep in tears, in anger, or in sheer bewilderment. They couldn't figure out why the outfit that they wore to work, or bought to look nice for their visit, or even that had been judged "acceptable" by a prison officer last week, wasn't permitted as visiting attire today. Over time, as I led them to the rack of donated, slightly misshapen, definitely outdated clothing and tried to help them find a garment close to their size, I began to think of the descriptions in Erving Goffman's *Asylums*. In this book, Goffman writes how inmates are "shaped and coded into an object that can be fed into the administrative machinery of the establishment, to be worked on smoothly by routine operations." This was particularly salient when a new visitor learned the ropes. The vibrant, chatty woman who arrived an hour early for her visit later had a face creased with anxiety when she returned with instructions to change out of her dress, became weepy when she was sent back a second time to borrow a soft-cup bra, and seemed melancholy and withdrawn when she finally returned to give us back the borrowed clothes. Social theorist Michel Foucault aptly described such processes as a dismantling of the self, a conversion into a "docile body" suited to carceral authority.

Eventually, my two years of employment at the visiting center became the practical guideposts for my dissertation fieldwork at San Quentin and the book that grew out of it, *Doing Time Together: Love and Family in the Shadow of the Prison.* As I deepened my observation and analysis of women's experiences maintaining contact with an incarcerated loved one, I discovered other parallels within the classic literature on inmates. I was inspired to return to sociologist Donald Clemmer's *The Prison Community*, particularly his concept of *prisonization*. Clemmer likens the prisonization of inmates to the Americanization of immigrants, describing it as the process of adapting to the correctional environment by learning the lingo, changing one's appearance and behavior, and generally "wising up" to the demands and expectations of the penal institution. Although the women I studied had more liberties than the men they were visiting, they, too, "wised up" to the penitentiary culture as they learned what clothes to wear (and the wisdom of bringing a spare outfit, just in case), which officer would cut them a break, how to get around the limit on the number of packages they could send to their loved one, and what time of day they could expect a collect call from the cell block. Through their contact with the prison, women with a loved one inside underwent "secondary prisonization"—a less potent but still powerful process derivative of and dependent upon the primary prisonization of the men they regularly visited.

The repercussive effects of the criminal justice system aren't limited to the United States. They have been studied in numerous countries, and they manifest differently according to political and cultural context. For example, sociologist Manuela da Cunha has examined women's incarceration in

Portugal, where the combination of scarce facilities for female prisoners and patterns of drug trade involvement in families has resulted in mothers, daughters, and sisters being locked up together. Without enough female family members left to care for children on the outside, the younger generation is brought into the prison. They live with the women while they serve their sentences, giving new meaning to the concept of a "family unit." Comparative and international research on incarceration's impact on family and social life highlights each country's peculiarities, but it also stimulates thinking about potential policy alternatives.

prison as a "domestic satellite"

In my fieldwork, I saw how women's adaptation to San Quentin helped them navigate the shifting dictates and arbitrary rules of the prison. However, it also blurred the line between women's private and prison spheres, at times creating a seamless crossover between the two. For instance, women who couldn't afford a separate wardrobe of prison-specific outfits started to consider, "Can I wear this into San Quentin?" before purchasing any new item of clothing. In time, their everyday clothes were "penitentiary clothes," conforming to the regulations imposed by the correctional authorities. Likewise, women learned to organize their work, meals, child care, and social schedules around the prison's visiting days and hours, as well as the periods during the day when men were allowed to make phone calls. Their daily routines became synchronized with the institution's timetable, more attuned to administrative requirements than the comfort and convenience of non-incarcerated women and children.

Distinctions between private and prison life eroded further for those women who tried to keep their loved ones closely involved in the rhythms of family life by "relocating" meals, celebrations, and other meaningful activities into the San Quentin visiting areas. Food often became a focal point, and women adjusted meal times to eat with their loved one during visits, even though this required making do with the expensive junk food available from the prison vending machines. For special occasions, visitors taught each other how to make "cakes" with vending machine items—for instance, by frosting a cinnamon roll with the cream cheese that came with a bagel and topping it with a chocolate bar melted in the microwave. Sometimes women tried to share meals prepared in their own kitchens: one Thanksgiving, a woman pressed turkey, stuffing, and side dishes into sandwich bags, concealed the bags in her pantyhose under loose trousers, and surreptitiously reassembled the feast in the visiting room before serving it to her husband.

Although these creative efforts were perhaps more pleasant than being forced to change clothes or think about San Quentin's regulations before buying a new shirt, they still demonstrate how women undergo secondary prisonization by having sustained, close contact with the penitentiary. The women transformed the prison into a "domestic satellite" in which family life was enacted. This, in turn, shifted women's expectations and actions over time, to the point that those who had long histories of visiting incarcerated loved ones expressed how the prison began to feel like "home."

seeking quality time

The notion that the penitentiary feels like home carries certain logic for those who spend twenty-four hours a day, seven days a week for years or decades behind bars. But it requires deeper analysis when non-incarcerated people say the same. Listening to women talk about what felt "homey" to them and was enjoyable about their visits emphasized how they had learned how to navigate San Quentin's rules, become accustomed to its routines and requirements, appreciate the limited sociability it anchored, and create moments of levity, celebration, and togetherness within and around its walls.

Finding out about the conditions of women's lives *away* from the prison added another dimension, showing how deeply the criminal justice system infiltrates the lives of the poor. Women told me how they and their children lived with fear, uncertainty, and anxiety in neighborhoods replete with violence. Some women visitors were homeless; others resided in cramped quarters without adequate space or beds for everyone. Many women worked long hours, often covering the night shift, worrying about the children they had to leave unattended. These portraits of outside lives were filled with cumulative economic hardships, a striking lack of social services, and unrelenting neighborhood violence. They shed light on the sense of *reprieve* women had when they visited San Quentin: in contrast to the danger and tumult of their everyday existences, having a place to sit down in safety, share a sandwich with a loved one, and hold a leisurely conversation while watching their kids play in the corner made women feel like they were taking a break.

One further distinction women underscored between their "inside" and "outside" lives were the changes they saw in their loved ones during incarceration. Many visitors spoke candidly about their partner's, son's, brother's, and friend's struggles with alcoholism, drug use, and mental health issues, and how there was nowhere to turn for help in their neighborhoods. In the absence of treatment programs or social workers they could turn to on the outside, men's problems often would escalate to the point that they were destabilizing and even dangerous for their families. Paradoxically, then, men's incarceration provided a sort of "relief" in that it eased the burden for sheltering, feeding, and managing the behavior of difficult men who needed, but couldn't get, professional help.

In addition, the men typically showed appreciation to those who took the time and spent the money necessary to keep in touch. Prisoners are highly constrained in what they can give to others: they make little or no money, and even hugs and kisses (let alone sex) are restricted. The gift of communication thus became the primary means by which men reciprocated women's caretaking: they listened attentively, asked questions, remembered details, talked for hours during visits and phone calls, and wrote frequent and lengthy letters in which they expressed their emotions and affirmed their commitment. Women remarked on the difference between men who were "ripping and running" on the streets, with little time or inclination to exchange a word, and those same men eagerly engaging in long, in-depth dialogue when they were in San Quentin. Although women at times felt cynical or sorrowful about the circumstances surrounding these transformations, they acknowledged that, without more economic, social, and psychological support structures in their neighborhoods, visiting rooms would continue to be the main places they could spend "quality time" with their loved ones. Prison was seemingly the only institution that could provide these women and their families with the stabilizing—if also degrading—support they needed.

no release in sight

Secondary prisonization helps us understand how people who maintain close relationships with prisoners can become "quasi-inmates" as they learn and respond to the constraints and dictates of a correctional facility. When visitors must completely reorganize their social and family lives around the rhythms of prison life, their efforts to maintain close ties with loved ones intensify the process of secondary prisonization. Prisons play a critical role in this process, but so too does the dearth of social and economic support outside of prison walls—support that might keep people *out* of prison and feeling safer, healthier, and less stressed within the walls of their own homes. This article hardly begins to address how dramatically one person's incarceration affects the lives of those to whom he or she is connected.

RECOMMENDED READING

Donald Clemmer. 1958 (1940). *The Prison Community* (2nd edition), San Francisco, CA: Rinehart. The classic text introducing the concept of "prisonization."

Megan Comfort. 2007. "Punishment Beyond the Legal Offender," *Annual Review of Law and Social Science* 3(1):271–296. A review of studies on the kinship webs and social networks of those subject to criminal punishment.

Lauren E. Glaze and Laura M. Maruschak. 2010. *Parents in Prison and Their Minor Children*, Washington, DC: Bureau of Justice Statistics Special Report. A brief statistical portrait of incarcerated parents and their children.

Erving Goffman. 1961. *Asylums: Essays on the Social Situation of Mental Patients and Other Inmates*, Garden City, NY: Doubleday. A pathbreaking analysis of "total institutions" and the social life of mental patients.

Loïc Wacquant. 2010. "Class, Race & Hyperincarceration in Revanchist America," *Daedalus* 139(3):74–90. Shows how social class, race, and place affect and distort the U.S. criminal justice system, leading to the disproportionate incarceration of African American men from impoverished neighborhoods.

TSP tie-in

the logic of our sex laws

Has a librarian ever "shushed" you for chatting in a quiet study area? As Howard Becker defined it in his book *Outsiders,* deviance is not the surreptitious talk but the librarian's reaction to your violation of a formal or informal rule. Becker's definition emphasizes the social construction of deviance and its ability to *change*; behaviors that were once deemed deviant may become legitimate practice (and vice versa) as boundaries of social acceptability are redrawn. For example, tattoos are so common, you can now see "Tattoos for Tots" on Sociological Images (go to thesocietypages.org/crime for a link).

While laws are not the only rules that construct accepted standards for behavior, they are codified norms that detail what society (or more precisely, those "moral entrepreneurs"— in Becker's terms--who have a hand in making and enforcing laws) deem unacceptable. So one way to observe shifting notions of deviance is to look at legal changes, particularly those surrounding what constitutes deviant sexual behavior.

For instance, in the 1970s, feminist scholar Catherine MacKinnon argued that the first step to rendering men's victimization of women visible was to redefine "normal," socially accepted behaviors as deviant. Accordingly, MacKinnon labeled acts including unwelcome or coercive sexual behaviors—the kind any episode of *Mad Men* will show you were common even in the workplace—"sexual harassment." Since the '70s, redefinitions have led to the construction and criminalization of even more forms of gender violence (committed against both women *and* men). By naming and mounting substantial legal mobilization, people have redefined behaviors that were once tolerated under the law as deviant.

The boundaries of social acceptability vary relative to both time and place, yet some research suggests that legal changes follow worldwide trends. For instance, David John Frank and his colleagues studied legal changes in the regulation of sex (namely rape, adultery, sodomy, and child sexual abuse) across the globe since 1945. Most countries have increased criminalization for rape and child sexual abuse and eliminated laws regulating adultery and sodomy, and most changes have followed the same trend, moving from emphasizing the protection of groups (e.g., criminalizing rape as an offense against the family) to the protection of individuals (e.g., criminalizing rape as an offense against any victim).

For a recent and visual example of redrawn boundaries of social acceptability, compare the maps of same-sex marriage laws across the United States before and after the 2012 election, posted on this volume's Web site.

SUZY MCELRATH

8

international criminal justice, with susanne karstedt, naomi roht-arriaza, wenona rymond-richmond, and kathryn sikkink

SHANNON GOLDEN AND HOLLIE NYSETH BREHM

I n our lifetimes, institutions like the International Criminal Court (ICC) have fundamentally reshaped the sphere of international justice and accountability. Just a few decades ago, an international criminal indictment against a sitting head of state would have been much less likely or perhaps even inconceivable. Today, the president of Sudan is wanted by the ICC.

The ICC traces much of its legacy back to the Nuremberg Trials, which held dozens of leaders of Nazi Germany accountable for their actions after World War II. Since then, temporary international tribunals have been created to respond to specific situations of mass atrocity and human rights abuses, such as in Rwanda or the former Yugoslavia. Some of these tribunals are still in place today, but they have been joined by the ICC, the world's first permanent, global court with jurisdiction over crimes seen as so egregious they are deemed crimes against all people.

We asked four leading experts to weigh in on some of the most controversial issues facing international criminal justice, including its potential interference with state sovereignty and its capacity to really curb human rights abuses.

Is the social control of crime at the international level a new development?

Naomi Roht-Arriaza: War crimes trials go back at least to the fourteenth century. Even the principle that some crimes are so heinous and so difficult for any one state to try has a long and storied pedigree, going back to cases involving piracy and slave trading.

Two things *are* perhaps new. . . . One is a commitment by states, at least in terms of discourse, to combat the impunity of powerful actors, whether they be heads of state, militia leaders, or generals. This is where national criminal law has had difficulty in many states. It is why international tribunals or prosecutions are sometimes necessary. The new salience of fighting impunity is a change driven by civil society—human rights groups, journalists, family members of victims, lawyers, women's groups, religious organizations, and others.

The second is the convergence of international *criminal* law with international *humanitarian* law (the law of war) and international *human rights* law. The kinds of crimes that international criminal law is predominantly concerned with—genocide, crimes against humanity, war crimes, torture, enforced disappearance, piracy, slavery, and the like—are also almost all violations of the law of war when committed during armed conflict. And, in addition to individual criminal responsibility, they are violations of human rights for which states are responsible if they commit, condone, or fail to protect against them.

Susanne Karstedt: Moving control of mass atrocity crimes to the international level has been a long process with numerous setbacks. . . . The Nuremberg Trials after World War II became a landmark of international criminal justice. Notwithstanding its numerous flaws, [Nuremberg] has become a benchmark for later trials, like Yugoslavia, Rwanda, and Cambodia. Regional initiatives and institutions [have also] had an undisputable impact, particularly in Europe and Latin America.

However, social control comprises more than formal institutions of criminal justice. It includes the reactions of communities toward crimes and offenders. Did social control in this sense move to the international level? Social control in the international sphere is highly dispersed among numerous institutions outside of the system of criminal justice, and [it is] based on regional and global power relations. A global civil society is emerging, with cosmopolitan actors and international NGOs actively working in the human rights regime and in crisis areas. . . .

Kathryn Sikkink: One of the great paradoxes of criminal law in the past was that if an ordinary criminal killed one person, there was a strong chance that he would be prosecuted and sent to prison, but if a state leader ordered the murder of thousands, he would virtually never be held accountable. Thus, the expansion of criminal law to include state officials addresses a glaring inequality in the criminal law system. However, the great bulk of such accountability is happening in domestic courts, not in the international tribunals. [So] the key issue is not the emergence of international criminal law by itself. Rather, the big issue is the emergence of an interrelated but decentralized system of accountability for core human rights violations that includes international, foreign, and domestic prosecutions and courts. Many of these domestic prosecutions primarily use domestic criminal law, not international criminal law. But international criminal law and international tribunals have played a key backup or supporting role in the process, both by producing some important legal innovations that have facilitated domestic trials and by making it more difficult for former state officials to escape accountability by going into exile.

International law is sometimes seen as a direct contradiction to the carefully protected principle of state sovereignty, or the idea that states have control of their own affairs. How do you see this developing in the future?

Roht-Arriaza: Much of international law is, in fact, an embodiment of the principle of state sovereignty. States freely negotiate and choose to enter into treaties with other states. With some exceptions, they can choose not to comply with specific treaty provisions they disagree with, while still being part of the treaty. States, through their practice and behavior, create implicit rules that over time become accepted as customary international law—if states don't like the emerging rule, they won't be bound by it if they persistently object to it. There are a few exceptions: A handful of norms, such as a prohibition on genocide or crimes against humanity, are considered inherent to state-dom, and therefore cannot be changed via treaty or through persistent objection.

So, it's not international law in itself that creates a challenge to state sovereignty. The international human rights regime does have a normative component, deriving from the inherent dignity of the individual, which says that people have rights whether their government chooses to recognize those rights or not. While we may disagree around the edges about what those rights are and how they are enforced, at the core there is little disagreement.

Sikkink: States use their capacity as sovereign states to ratify human rights treaties that essentially "invite" other states and international organizations to intervene in issues that were previously considered internal affairs. This process is so far advanced that it begins to seem naïve for states to later complain that their sovereignty is being undermined. When I see states that have ratified multiple human rights treaties with detailed provisions for international supervision of human rights practices later complain about violations of sovereignty, I always think of the scene from the film *Casablanca* where the corrupt police inspector says that he is "shocked, shocked, to find that gambling is going on here" at the same time as he accepts the cash winnings for bets he has placed. In other words, states ratify treaties hoping to gain something, perhaps international legitimacy, and then later claim that they are "shocked" to find that the fine print of the treaty may actually be implemented.

Karstedt: State sovereignty is indeed crucial to the success and proliferation of international criminal justice. Nonetheless, with the establishment of international criminal tribunals, the international community has taken bold steps toward restraining sovereignty. In particular, the principles of the responsibility to protect and to prosecute restrict sovereignty are often seen as direct and imminent threats to it. For example, as the international crime of genocide justifies (military) intervention ... any definition of a situation as genocide can be seen as an invitation to intervene directly into sovereign states.

Roht-Arriaza: It is also true that some states are more sovereign than others in practice: It is far easier to bring international criminal charges against a militia leader in the Congo than against Donald Rumsfeld. And international law can, and often is, used to enforce and expand the power of powerful states. This, it seems to me, is not a problem unique to international criminal law, but rather shows the limits of law itself when confronted with power.

The International Criminal Court is often hailed as the culmination of decades of work promoting international law and individual criminal accountability. Looking back on the ICC's first 10 years, how do you assess its contributions and achievements?

Wenona Rymond-Richmond: Decades of work promoting international law and individual criminal accountability culminated in the establishment of the ICC. . . . Contributions and achievements of the Court include a warrant [for the arrest of] Sudanese president Omar al-Bashir: Charges filed by former Chief Prosecutor Luis Moreno-Ocampo against President Bashir include war crimes, crimes against humanity, genocide, rape, and mass murder as genocide. Of these charges, rape as genocide is the most groundbreaking. Prosecuting the crime of rape as genocide is unprecedented for the ICC and relies on two lesser-known ways of destroying a people, as stated in the Genocide Convention: "causing serious bodily or mental harm to members of the group" or "deliberately inflicting on the group conditions of life calculated to bring about its physical destruction in whole or in part." Prosecuting President Bashir.... will provide a legal precedence for the Court to pursue rape as a form of genocide in the future.

Additional contributions and achievements of the ICC include the conviction of Lubanga Dyilo [the first person convicted by the ICC, found guilty of conscripting child soldiers], the issuance of 22 warrants of arrest, the overseeing of 16 cases in seven countries, and the investigation of seven ongoing situations. Furthermore, the ICC has [created] an unprecedented series of rights for the victims to present their experience before the Court and established a trust fund to make financial reparations to victims. In this way, the ICC possesses an extraordinary opportunity to bridge the gap between retributive and restorative justice.

Karstedt: Defining the International Criminal Court as the "culmination" of decades of development of international criminal justice seems to raise expectations to a very high level. Indeed, the ICC presently suffers from exaggerated expectations. I would suggest seeing the ICC as part of a process of continuous proliferation of legal instruments and institutions that deal with mass atrocity crimes and human rights violations. In the course of this process, numerous local, regional, and international institutions have emerged. Rather than being the apex of this buildup, the ICC should be seen as part of it, connected in various ways to local and regional forms of justice and peacemaking. Whether justice will cascade down from the ICC . . . as a model or whether [the Court] will be invigorated and changed by local initiatives, we do not know yet.

Roht-Arriaza: The creation of the ICC was an enormous achievement, but it also created unrealistic expectations that the ICC—or any court—could single-handedly do away with mass atrocity. There have been legitimate criticisms of the ICC: it is very slow, the prosecutor has at times been willing to cut corners or has pursued too narrow a strategy. . . . The decision to focus on only African situations, while perhaps responding to . . . the constraints of the Rome Statute that limits who the ICC can investigate, has created frictions with African states. It has showed that the Achilles' heel of the ICC, and of international justice in general, is the need to rely on state cooperation to actually detain suspects. Thus, when Sudan's president Al-Bashir, wanted by the ICC, can still travel internationally and not be immediately arrested, the ICC's long-term credibility is undermined, and, when the UN Security Council hears about the failure to cooperate and does nothing about it, the problem is compounded.

Sikkink: It is still very early . . . if we compare [the ICC] to other important regional human rights courts, like the European Court of Human Rights or the Inter-American Court of Human Rights, we see that [other courts] did relatively little in their first ten years. Both [of these] courts have gone on to produce many landmark cases, but [not] in their first decades. The ICC has succeeded in setting itself up, surviving, and moving ahead with its tasks—far more than many predicted, given the initial harsh opposition from the United States. The initial prediction was that the United States would make sure the Court was never able to function properly. Instead, the United States, even during the Bush administration, was obliged to change its position from active hostility to tacit acceptance.

Second, in order to evaluate the achievements of the Court, we don't only want to assess what happens in The Hague, but the effectiveness of the whole "Rome Statute system." The Rome Statute, which established the ICC, set forth the doctrine of complementarity, meaning that the ICC is a last resort when national courts have failed. . . . One important goal of the ICC is to work with states to modify their laws . . . and to develop their capacity to prosecute genocide, crimes against humanity, and war crimes in domestic courts. Thus, one underappreciated part of the work of the Court has been the degree to which it has spurred domestic legislative changes and prosecutions.

Some argue that international trials deter future human rights abuses. Do they? What are some other important effects of such trials?

Karstedt: As a criminologist, I am rather skeptical of criminal justice being a deterrent in general. First, even domestically, there is hardly any reliable evidence of a deterrent impact of criminal justice, neither on the individual offender, given the enormous recidivism rates, nor on the community, as high imprisonment rates do not seem to have a substantive impact on crime levels. Second, it is important to unpack the *concept* of deterrence: Does this imply that perpetrators are deterred from re-offending or that non-offenders are deterred from committing a crime? As French sociologist Émile Durkheim pointed out, the function of punishment is not the prevention of crime but the confirmation and validation of norms. Punishment thus enhances the solidarity of communities as their members rally around the visible demonstration and "monumental spectacle" of reactions to breaking rules, norms, and laws.

Indeed, the threat of prosecution may weigh little against what might appear to be gained in a conflict situation. Notwithstanding, the normative appeal of international criminal justice to "put an end to impunity" has emerged as a powerful tool. Both globally and regionally, mass atrocity crimes and human rights violations have subsided; it cannot be proven whether deterrence as threat of punishment or as normative change and confirmation of norms was actually decisive in this process. I would rather opt for the latter than for the former.

Roht-Arriaza: This is, empirically, very hard to prove—it's the "dog that didn't bark" problem. How do we know how many human rights abuses were deterred? We do have some anecdotal evidence that leaders of murderous regimes are afraid to be "sent to The Hague," but that's about it.

However, trials do serve other important purposes . . . they help stem revisionist history and establish facts, they allow victims and survivors to visualize the change in power that put the once all-powerful [on trial], and, sometimes, [they can let victims] confront [perpetrators]. Trials can, in this sense, rebalance power and head off vigilante justice and collective blame. They can also incapacitate, either through incarceration or political discrediting, local leaders who would otherwise continue to wield power, to terrorize, and to impede any change to a more just society. They can signal the emergence of norms of behavior, and help set the limits of the thinkable—and the unthinkable. And yet . . . trials are necessary but never sufficient.

Sikkink: International trials are still too few and too recent to give any systematic judgment about their effects. . . . But some of my research shows that human rights prosecutions, including combinations of both international and domestic trials, are associated with improvements in human rights practices in transitional countries. This suggests that trials, including international trials, may indeed deter human rights abuses. . . . The most complex issue with determining the effects of international trials is that such trials are carried out in exactly those countries with the most severe situations, including conflict, authoritarianism, and chaos. This creates some selection effects. . . .

Rymond-Richmond: I agree with fellow roundtable panelists that it is challenging to prove that international trials deter human rights abuse because far too few have occurred.... Yet, there are indications that legal interventions more broadly can deter future human rights abuses. One of the best and most creative examples is Savelsberg and King's 2011 book *American Memories.* [These authors have done] a remarkable job of demonstrating that legal intervention may be a key mechanism in curtailing ... mass atrocities. In addition, trials play an important role in shaping a nation's collective memory of past atrocities and shaping present-day laws against hate-motivated violence.

Citing the potential benefits, advocates claim trials are essential in the wake of human rights abuses. Others argue that resources would be better used for more far-reaching measures, like truth commissions or reparations. In the broader context of post-conflict rebuilding, what do you think is the role of criminal trials of individual perpetrators in dealing with widespread situations?

Sikkink: Why are transitional justice choices so often framed in either/or terms? It does not and should not have to be a choice among truth commissions, reparations, and trials. In fact, many countries use all three. . . . Different transitional justice mechanisms serve different purposes. Until we know more about what works . . . I would not say that criminal trials are somehow [more or] less capable of addressing these situations than other mechanisms.

Karstedt: International trials are defining moments for societies emerging from a violent past. They symbolize the end to impunity for individual perpetrators and set the scene for further prosecution in years to come. For example, it was a common criticism of the Auschwitz trials that only a handful of perpetrators were brought to justice. . . . However, [it] was a "cultural watershed" for German society, for the first time, the voices of the victims could be heard.

Roht-Arriaza: If all that is done is to try a few perpetrators, trials may be necessary but not sufficient to dealing with the aftermath of mass atrocity. What's needed is a holistic effort to [re]construct social relations and political trust. . . . This may involve a wide array of measures, including truth telling, documentation and archival work, reparations, revamping and cleansing of government services, memorialization, changes in educational curriculum, and more. Over the last few years, that agenda has broadened even more, so that we're now including in the idea of "transitional justice" efforts to deal with the marginalization of groups. . . . While the needs will be similar, how each state does this will differ depending on their culture, traditions, the nature of the conflict, and so on. It will have to be done, moreover, with close attention to not reproducing earlier oppressions—of women, of indigenous peoples—and to ensuring that those most affected have a say.

International criminal justice has changed tremendously over the last several decades. Based on what we have seen, do you have any predictions (or hopes) about its future?

Sikkink: The main issue is not the future of international criminal justice but the future of the interrelated but decentralized system of accountability for human rights violations (which includes international and domestic prosecutions). With regard to this system of accountability, the most striking theme in my book *The Justice Cascade* is the persistence of the demand for justice: I believe human rights prosecutions will not go away. Such prosecutions are not a panacea for all the ills of society, and they will inevitably disappoint as they fall short of our ideals. They represent an advance, however, over the complete lack of accountability of the past, and they have the potential to prevent human rights violations in the future.

Roht-Arriaza: Our expectations of international criminal justice will eventually come more into line with what it can actually accomplish. It can't put societies back together, it can't bring closure to those who have suffered horrible losses, and it can't rid the world of international crime, any more than domestic courts have been able to abolish ordinary crimes. It *can* make modest contributions to each of these things, and that's all to the good. I think we will see new ways of intertwining international and national prosecutions, supporting the national courts, [and] linking reparations and structural reform to justice efforts. And I think that we will see new kinds of conflicts over natural resources and land, which will require their own set of holistic responses.

Rymond-Richmond: My hopes . . . include continued and increased global support of the International Criminal Court. The ICC has the potential to contribute to world peace and security. However, international criminal justice is only one piece of [the] holistic approach necessary to eliminate human rights violations. [This] includes identifying precursors to mass atrocities, increased international and national prosecutions, assistance and protection for refugees and internally displaced people, raising the status of women, eliminating racial and ethnic discrimination, understanding the context of genocide, and [funding] reparations for victims.

We must try, through a variety of means, including scholarship, activism, and legal interventions, to end the massive killing, raping, and displacement that has left a scar on the twentieth century and each century before. What is the alternative? For individuals, states, or the international community to be bystanders to atrocities is shameful and the implications of inactivity are deadly. Advancements in international criminal justice are a step in the right direction.

Karstedt: The development and proliferation of international criminal justice testifies to the human capability of inventing institutions—good ones as well as bad ones that do a lot of harm. . . . Its history also testifies to the many obstacles and setbacks that international criminal justice has to confront. It is my hope that international criminal justice becomes the beacon for institutions all over the world to end impunity for human rights violations and mass atrocities, and that it promotes the empowerment of citizens to find their own ways out of conflicts and violence.

PARTICIPANT PROFILES

Susanne Karstedt is in the School of Law at the University of Leeds. Her present research is on violent societies, mass atrocities and genocide, with particular expertise on the Holocaust trials in post-war Germany. She is the editor of *Legal Institutions and Collective Memories* (Hart Publishing, 2010).

Naomi Roht-Arriaza is in the Hastings College of the Law at the University of California. She specializes in accountability for human rights violations and is the author of *The Pinochet Effect: Transnational Justice in the Age of Human Rights* (University of Pennsylvania Press, 2005).

Wenona Rymond-Richmond is in the department of sociology at the University of Massachusetts, Amherst. Her research focuses on genocide, race and ethnicity, and sociology of law. She is co-author (with John Hagan) of *Darfur and the Crime of Genocide* (Cambridge University Press, 2008).

Kathryn Sikkink is in the department of political science at the University of Minnesota. She studies international human rights law, transnational advocacy networks, and international politics and is the author of *The Justice Cascade (The Chicago Journal of International Law)*.

9

the crime of genocide

HOLLIE NYSETH BREHM

R ain pelted the side of the empty school building, drown-
ing out all other sounds. In the distance I could see
lightning strike across the rolling green hills. The
weather couldn't have fit the situation better. For even though
the classrooms were vacant, they were far from empty—they
held the corpses of over 800 people killed in the 1994 genocide perpetrated against Tutsis in Rwanda. Mothers, fathers,
sisters, brothers—even babies—lay on tables where students'
desks might have stood. Some held flowers, likely put there
by memorial staff; others clutched rosaries, perhaps left
from their last moments.

The faces of the bodies in the Murambi Genocide Memorial in southwestern Rwanda will haunt me. Some faces were
twisted in pain or frozen in a scream; others were obscured
by arms held up in defense against their killers. Even worse
is knowing that the memorial is just one of many places
where people were slaughtered during the genocide, which

claimed roughly one million lives over the course of several months.

How could people do this to one another? This question guides the studies of many genocide scholars. Because even more disturbing than the Murambi Memorial is the fact that the genocide in Rwanda is not a unique event. As much as we would like to think otherwise, genocide has taken place multiple times over the last several decades. In fact, by the calculations of sociologist Joachim Savelsberg, among others, more people died as a result of genocide than as a result of all murders, homicides, and manslaughters that took place during the twentieth century, one reason some criminologists think of genocide as the "crime of crimes."

the "crime of crimes"

The term *genocide* was coined in the wake of the Nazi Holocaust, making it a relatively new crime in terms of social definition. A Jewish Polish lawyer named Rafael Lemkin created the term by combining the Greek word *genos,* which means people or nation, and the Latin suffix *–cide,* which means murder. Lemkin lobbied tirelessly for this newly named crime to be recognized as such at the international level. After several years, the United Nations adopted the term, first in the form of a resolution and then in a convention (a binding treaty for all that ratify it). The eventual treaty, often called the Genocide Convention, took force on December 9, 1948. Drawing upon Lemkin's definition, the Convention explains genocide as "the intent to destroy, in whole or in part, a national, ethnic, racial, or religious group, as such. . . ." This destruction often, if not always, involves mass killings, though it also can involve other forms of victimization, such as rape or forcibly transferring children.

This definition was also adopted in several international tribunals and in the 1998 Rome Charter, which established the International Criminal Court, further solidifying genocide as a crime under international law. Many scholars disagree with elements of this definition (e.g., some argue that political groups should also be included), and the debate could fill pages. What's important to know is that scholars generally agree that genocide involves the intent to destroy a social group.

While the Genocide Convention is associated with the catchphrase "Never Again," genocides have continued. Some captured international attention and are commonly recognized as genocides by activists and scholars (like the genocide perpetrated against the Tutsi in Rwanda or the Khmer Rouge's genocide in present-day Cambodia), while other genocides are less widely recognized, in part because their classification *as* genocides is debated.

Yet, despite the magnitude and prevalence of this crime, *criminologists* had, until recently, largely neglected the study of genocide. Perhaps this is because genocide is often seen as a unique crime. While genocide cannot be equated with other crimes, it does share certain elements in common with them. For example, its high rate of participation is shared by crimes like speeding and shoplifting, while its temporal instability is akin to that of terrorism or rioting. Similarly, the targeting of people because they belong (or are seen as belonging) to a group is found in hate crimes, while the involvement of the state in genocide can be compared to crimes like nuclear weapon possession. More comparisons could be made, but the general point is this: genocide is a crime, and while other crimes cannot be equated with genocide, they are comparable along various aspects. This is why sociologists like Joachim Savelsberg, John Hagan, Wenona Rymond-Richmond, and Alexander Alvarez are today viewing genocide through the lens of criminology.

There are myriad ways that theories from criminology could inform genocide studies, which typically do not focus on the criminal nature of genocide. Indeed, criminology holds great potential for understanding genocide. And in turn, the scope conditions of well-established criminological theories can be tested on the crime of genocide, which can also contribute to genocide studies. Such interdisciplinary pursuits could inform the study of what genocide is, why it occurs, how it unfolds, and how it is punished, both locally and internationally. In what follows, I focus mainly on understanding why the crime of genocide takes place and also briefly cover responses to genocide.

preconditions of genocide

"Genocide doesn't come like rain," a Rwandan government official told me. That is, it isn't unpredictable like the rainy season's random downpours; instead, years of discrimination and planning precede genocide. It is very complex, involving a combination of many factors that result in a distinct social situation in which genocide might take place. Scholars in several disciplines, including history and political science, have identified a number of these factors, ranging from psychological to societal and state factors and, more recently, international ones. Some of these factors are briefly considered below, but it is important to note that these categories are not strict—they are, instead, meant to help organize the intricacy. In addition, none of the factors listed are *sufficient* to cause genocide. Rather, genocides occur due to a confluence of factors.

PSYCHOLOGICAL AND INDIVIDUAL FACTORS

It's tempting to think those who perpetrate genocide are psychologically deranged. However, in psychological studies, the most enduring finding is that people who commit genocide are "normal." This finding stems from several experiments, such as Stanley Milgram's well-known studies of obedience, in which Milgram sought whether "psychologically average" people would shock others at lethal levels. Almost everyone complied with his requests to shock others when he varied situational factors, such as the proximity of an authority (the researcher) or the presence of someone else who verbally refused to administer shocks. Milgram's experiments showed that the situation and context matter.

Genocide scholars have extended these findings to argue that the actions of most people who perpetrate genocide are subject to social constraints and influence—the perpetrators are not psychologically ill. In her study of the trial of Adolf Eichmann, responsible for the deportation of Jews during the Holocaust, political theorist Hannah Arendt noted that Eichmann was disturbingly normal. Other social scientists have profiled people who participated in genocide and noted that, in terms of age, occupation, and even family life, they seemed "average." In addition, recent examination by criminologists has begun to show that even "average" follows certain social patterns, though. For example, Christopher Uggen, Jean-Damascène Gasanabo, and I are currently studying the age and sex of those who participated in the Rwandan genocide. By and large, we find that the perpetrators were overwhelmingly men, and while they were generally older than people who commit other crimes (like homicide), their ages follow an age-crime curve like that of many other crimes. This illustrates that the individual determinants of crime also matter in the case of genocide.

While the actions of perpetrators are subject to social constraints, perpetrators are not without agency. Many genocide scholars focus on the key role played by certain individuals in planning and implementing the events of a genocide, often highlighting the extreme ideologies that motivate their actions. Nevertheless, while individuals and their actions are key to understanding genocide, neither can be understood without social context.

SOCIETAL AND GROUP FACTORS

Many times, news media portray genocide as a result of tribal warfare and ethnic conflict. A number of scholars have looked closely at the makeup of societies that experience genocide, and some do believe that more diverse societies are more likely to experience genocide—the "diversity breeds conflict" argument. Other research, including my own, has shown the opposite: diverse societies are *not* more prone to genocide. Instead, how diversity is reflected in the structures of society matters. For example, Barbara Harff, a political scientist, shows that societies in which the ethnicity of rulers is a point of contention are more likely to experience genocide. Thus, in Rwanda, the Hutus controlled the government in the years prior to the country's genocide, while Tutsis were excluded from virtually all positions of power. Not only did this inequity result in power struggles and civil war, it instilled a deep-seated ideology of difference and mistrust within the society.

Genocide has always been perpetrated by more than one person, so social scientific research on groups is relevant. As Joachim Savelsberg notes, Edwin Sutherland's classic ideas about learning to commit crime in groups can be applied to genocide. These ideas can be extended, since societal-wide "learning" in genocides often takes place through propaganda campaigns to dehumanize certain groups, and they can be considered in terms of singular acts (researchers have found, for instance, that people learn both to commit and *how* to commit torture in groups).

Criminologists John Hagan and Wenona Rymond-Richmond have also drawn upon theories of collective action and crime to understand why genocide took place in the Darfur region of Sudan at the beginning of the twenty-first century. Utilizing James Coleman's macro/micro scheme, they make explicit connections between the social condition of genocide and individual acts of aggression, like using racial epithets or ethnic slurs. They begin at the macro level by noting resource competition and the Sudanese government's ideologies directed against certain tribes in Darfur. This provided a vocabulary that reinforced an us/them theme. At the micro level of personal interactions, this us/them dichotomy and vocabulary influenced racist attitudes and actions. This illustrates how individual actions can be transformed into collectivized racial intent, which is then aggregated to macro-level patterns of genocide through collective action and a genocidal state. Their theory shows how genocide unfolds at individual, group, and societal levels and highlights the interplay *between* these levels. It also points to the importance of another actor—the state.

STATE FACTORS

More often than not, societal-wide campaigns are implemented by agents of the state. As noted, Hagan and Rymond-Richmond found that the national-level government played a large role in generating ideologies directed against groups in the genocide in Darfur. These ideologies influenced socially constructed identities, provided a vocabulary that reinforced an "us versus them" theme, dehumanized groups of people, and eventually influenced the actions of individuals.

For this and several other reasons, many scholars believe that genocides cannot happen without the will and power of the state. Even if a state turns a blind eye, its inaction may lend authority to those perpetuating a genocide. Accordingly, studies have identified various characteristics of states that influence the occurrence of genocide. Upheaval (such as a civil war, regime change, or even resource scarcity) is, by far, one of the biggest predictors, perhaps owing to leaders' perceptions of threats to society-wide strain and uncertainty. The type of government also matters. Genocides don't tend to occur in democracies, in part due to government checks and balances and in part due to the freedoms associated with such societies. Genocides also usually don't occur in resource-rich countries, though this isn't necessarily the case (Nazi Germany was hardly resource poor).

In addition, states' colonial histories are an important part of the story, though the effects of colonialism are difficult to disentangle. They are reflected in many aspects of life. In the case of Rwanda, for example, sixty years before the 1994 genocide, colonial Belgium introduced identity cards based on ethnicity. The cards still affected daily life in the years leading up to the genocide. Lastly, the highly structured, modern bureaucratic nature of the state also influences the occurrence of genocide. As Max Weber noted, bureaucratization (the rationalization of processes through hierarchy, continuity, impersonality, and expertise) is a defining quality of modernity, and it has resulted in organizations and states that are able to reach their goals in a more effective manner. Efficacy can have a dark side.

international factors and responses

In recent years, genocide scholars have widened their lens to examine the international aspects of genocide. At one time, rulers could destroy swaths of people and be heralded as heroes and conquerors by many, while most other inhabitants remained ignorant of the conquest for years.

Today, the world is a much more interconnected place. The Genocide Convention itself illustrates that there are now global norms about what people and states can and cannot do. Interconnectedness reaches beyond ratifying treaties, though. States that remain interconnected through trading and membership in political organizations seem to have lower odds of genocide. The precise mechanisms for these effects are still understudied, but more and more social scientists are reinforcing this finding. Interstate relationships may create global checks and balances that rein in serious misconduct, in the same way democratic checks and balances seem to lower individual countries' chances of genocide. They create ally ties, so states have other countries to answer to (and for).

Global norms also matter for interventions in genocide. The 2005 World Summit proclaimed that states have a "Responsibility to Protect." Essentially, this means that states hold a primary obligation to protect their own citizens from genocide and other grave human rights violations. Since governments are often the perpetrators of these crimes, the "Responsibility to Protect" also holds that the international community has the responsibility to halt genocide and similar crimes if another state fails to protect—or actively endangers—its own population.

Even if we can now start to understand the situations and factors that combine to influence the occurrence of genocide, responding to (or even preventing) genocide is a different story. There are many potential responses to genocide, ranging from immediate intervention to try to halt the violence—like trade embargoes or armed intervention—to humanitarian aid aimed at alleviating immediate suffering. Of particular interest to criminologists, there are also judicial responses: courts were created after the genocides in Rwanda and the former Yugoslavia and, in 2002, the International Criminal Court (ICC) was created to prosecute perpetrators of genocide (often by applying standing legal logic in innovative ways). In fact, the president of Sudan is currently wanted by the ICC, accused of war crimes, crimes against humanity, and the genocide perpetrated in Darfur, a region in Western Sudan. In light of these developments, criminologists have started to study how these international courts operate, how they work with domestic courts, and their effects.

These only scratch the surface of potential responses to genocide, and responding to genocide itself is rather new. As you can guess, it's also quite political. *Who* has the authority to respond to genocide, whether it's an international government organization, a humanitarian organization, or even an individual country, is still heavily debated. Regardless, though, social science can inform responses to genocide and will be an important player in seeking to better understand this crime and effective responses.

Overall, it's not *easy* to understand why such a harrowing crime takes place, but it is possible. While genocide appeared to be utterly unpredictable, we now know that it is often a criminal response to a combination of psychological, societal, state, and even international factors. We still have a long way to go, but social scientific work represents enormous progress toward the ideal of a world that does not need any more memorials like the school in Murambi.

RECOMMENDED READING

Helen Fein. 1993. "Accounting for Genocide after 1945: Theories and Some Findings," *International Journal on Group Rights* 1(2):79–106. One of the first (and only) sociological studies of preconditions of genocide; many of its findings inform research conducted today.

John Hagan and Wenona Rymond-Richmond. 2009. *Darfur and the Crime of Genocide*. New York: Cambridge University Press. A powerful example of how social scientific research can be used to prove that genocide is taking place.

Barbara Harff. 2003. "No Lessons Learned from the Holocaust? Assessing Risks of Genocide and Political Mass Murder since 1955," *American Political Science Review* 97(1):57–73. The findings of this article are now used in global models predicting the occurrence of genocide.

Joachim J. Savelsberg. 2010. *Crime and Human Rights: Criminology of Genocide and Atrocities*. Thousand Oaks, CA: Sage. An accessible look at how criminology can inform (and learn from) the study of genocide and grave human rights violations.

Eric D. Weitz. 2003. *A Century of Genocide: Utopias of Race and Nation*. Princeton, NJ: Princeton University Press. Uses four cases to explain why the twentieth century saw some of the most systematic and deadly genocides.

critical takes

10

correcting american corrections, with francis cullen, david garland, david jacobs, and jeremy travis

SARAH LAGESON

n this Roundtable, a panel of experts reflect on a Pew Center on the States Survey that found half of Americans believe there are too many prisoners in the United States. The survey also found that voters believed that one fifth of prisoners could be released without compromising public safety. In other findings, 48% agreed with reducing funding for state prisons and large majorities favored reducing prison time for low-risk, nonviolent offenders.

Our Roundtable panelists, while encouraged by the implementation of this survey, were careful not to put too much positive spin on the results. Public support may be moving toward a less punitive America, but it's not certain policy will quickly follow suit.

We began by asking whether anything in the Pew results surprised our respondents. Their answers ranged from near dismissal to cautious optimism.

David Jacobs: There are only a few policies that respond to public opinion, so I'm not optimistic that these opinions matter much. The conventional wisdom in American politics in political science seems to be that public opinion drives policy. But that's only true about a few intensely moral issues. And if the issue is at all complicated, forget it because most citizens don't know much about politics. . . . Social scientists who don't specialize in politics often think in terms of a left-right continuum, but these categories aren't meaningful to most people. For example, if you ask people if they are conservative or liberal, you'll get answers. But if you correlate those ideological self-identifications with actual policy or voting, they don't seem to matter much. And if you ask the same people the same question later, you often get different answers, because most citizens don't seem to know what these ideological labels mean.

Frank Cullen: As someone who has studied public opinion for thirty years, I am not overly surprised by any of the findings. I am heartened that the survey was undertaken, however, because it shows that the American public holds reasonable views about crime-control policy. Its members realize that mass incarceration is not a sustainable policy and is not appropriate for all offenders.

Jeremy Travis: Perhaps the most important finding of the Pew survey was the bottom line—nearly half of those surveyed thought there were too many prisoners in America, and nearly half thought prison budgets could be reduced. For elected officials—and candidates for office—who have thought that the public would not support criminal justice reforms designed to reduce the size of our prison populations, these survey results should give them confidence in moving forward. What is more impressive however, are the survey findings that the public wants a more effective criminal justice system, not just a less expensive one. . . . The public official seeking to cut back on the levels of incarceration would be well advised to propose an alternative investment strategy for the savings—preferably one that would enhance the justice system.

David Garland: The American people are right to think that we punish too many people and we have too many people in prison. And it's good [to see in these results] that they've caught up with that fact. On the other hand, it's the American people and their representatives who have created that situation and my guess is that many American people polled in these opinion polls will say that we punish too many people for too long, but the *particular* offender who just burgled my house or raped my neighbor's daughter or robbed this store, *they* deserve never to be let out. . . . So there's a disjuncture sometimes between the abstract opinion and the particular one.

However, I have to say that I'm deeply pessimistic—to the point of being depressed—about the following fact: The mass imprisonment system that's been built up in America is one of world-historic proportions. No nation of any description (but certainly not a liberal democratic nation) has ever before had a carceral system in which 750 per 100,000 people are incarcerated. The equivalent in Europe is about a sixth of that, a seventh of that, sometimes a tenth of that, and I really don't see how the United States of America can move toward having normal rates of imprisonment in any time period that one can envisage. . . . The buildup has taken forty years. To get back to [our even comparatively high rates of incarceration in the '70s], it's hard to see how it can take less than forty years.

We then asked whether our experts could speculate as to the causes of the opinion shifts found in Pew's poll. Could we point to politics, economics, or cultural changes that might lead to a new outlook on crime and punishment?

Cullen: I do not believe that public opinion has shifted at all—or, in the least, that much. I think that what has shifted is the questions that are asked in the surveys. For example, public support for rehabilitation has remained high for three decades . . . the public has long made reasonable judgments. They want offenders who are dangerous to be incapacitated in prison. While they are there, they want efforts undertaken to rehabilitate them. They will support community-based sentences for many offenders, so long as this includes appropriate supervision and treatment. What they do not support is irresponsible decision making, where dangerous offenders are released inappropriately or where offenders are placed in the community with little intervention.

Jacobs: Crime rates are down, so maybe people aren't as threatened by [crime]. The Republicans also no longer campaign on law and order, probably because it doesn't work well anymore.

Garland: It has to be said that the remarkable diminution in crime rates, sustained over several decades now, has made crime less of an emergency, urgent, top-of-the-agenda issue for many people in this country. That's not to say that crime rates in this country are low: Homicide rates are still four or five times that of any other liberal democratic industrialized nation. On the other hand, crime is less pressing as an issue and crime rates have come down considerably. Our cities—many of them—are safer. Not *all* of them, but where I live in New York City, it's considerably safer. For these reasons, I think, the relaxation of punitive energy and enthusiasm is to be expected. The buildup of a massively extensive penal apparatus (prison system, jail system, probation system, parole system) in which there are 7.5 million people on a daily basis, that of course is an enormously expensive undertaking. And, at a time of fiscal stringency where teachers . . . and police officers are being laid off, of course politicians . . . and the public are beginning to consider [whether] we were a little extravagant in our use of penal resources and prisons and does everyone need to be in there forever?

Travis: The nation is witnessing a gradual shift in attitudes regarding our response to crime. The best indicator of this shift can be seen in our juvenile justice system. Twenty years ago, during the rise of juvenile violence in the 1980s, young people were demonized in our public discourse. Some experts said we were witnessing a generation of "super predators," and warned of a coming bloodbath. In this atmosphere, we passed laws severely punishing young people for their crimes. As a result, the number of youth in prison climbed to historic high levels. Now, we are witnessing a remarkable decline in the number of youth in detention and placement facilities. We are seeing a similar shift in public attitudes toward the death penalty, as 18 states have outlawed capital punishment, and the number of executions has dwindled.

Unfortunately, the winds of change have not yet swept our system of adult prisons. Granted, the nation has seen small declines in rates of incarceration and some states have seen their prison populations drop by as much as 20%, but we still incarcerate our population at rates far higher than any other country. The reason for these shifts? The decline in crime is the most important factor. . . . But there is another force at work—our crime policy is becoming more pragmatic, more focused on problems, less ideological. Community policing, problem-solving courts, the reentry movement, the emphasis on "best practices" and "evidence-based policies"—these developments hold great hope for the future. Finally, the nation is coming to grips with the deleterious effects of our criminal justice policies. The revelations of hundreds of wrongful convictions give us pause about the efficacy of the criminal justice system. And the heightened awareness of the devastating consequences of our justice system for communities of color provides a strong impetus to reduce the harms we cause.

When we turned to considering what actual changes in imprisonment policies, and even release programs, might mean for the public, Frank Cullen pointed out a historic parallel and its unintended consequences.

Cullen: The difficulty is in seeing prisons as the answer to the crime problem. Research is clear in showing that placing an offender in prison is not more effective in reducing future recidivism than a community-based penalty. Mostly, the savings that accrue from imprisonment is the crime saved while an offender is behind bars. Given this reality, it makes sense to imprison only high-risk offenders (or those whose crime is so serious that punishment by prison is deserved). A crucial issue is not simply who is or is not sent to prison but rather what else we do while an offender is within our grasp. Simply put, the correctional system should "correct." There is a growing literature on what works to rehabilitate offenders. . . .

Finally, a massive release of prisoners would, by itself, be irresponsible policy. To be responsible, we should, first of all, refrain from sending low-risk offenders to prison [in the first place]. Then, we should release . . . those offenders who are low risk—either because they were never high risk or because their risk levels have been lowered through treatment programs. [And], for those released after [serving their time], we should ensure that effective reentry programs are established . . . that they receive appropriate supervision that includes not only surveillance but also treatment.

We do not wish to repeat the errors that occurred when patients in mental hospitals were deinstitutionalized in mass numbers—too often [they were released to lives of] no services and, for too many, to lives of despair and/or homelessness. Anything we do in the criminal justice system should be done responsibly.

Travis, too, urged cautious, carefully planned changes in carceral policy.

Travis: Advocates for lower levels of incarceration have often said, "Now the prison system has finally gotten too expensive, and our elected officials will finally see the error of their ways and reduce the prison population." For forty years, this prediction has not been borne out. On the contrary, . . . in the face of ever-expanding prison populations and corrections budgets, our elected officials have been willing to pay the bill. And they have been supported by the public.

These survey results do not help public officials consider the potential costs and benefits of a program of large-scale releases of prisoners [because] the questions in this survey are based on various policy alternatives and assume the policymaker is operating in a world of considered decisions. A large-scale release program poses enormous risks . . . the near certainty that someone released early will commit a serious crime. Perhaps the public will be understanding and recognize that this crime could also have occurred at a later date, when the release was originally scheduled. But, more likely, the public will view this as a crime that [would] not have occurred, and will hold the government official responsible. So early release programs should be considered with great caution. This concern also argues for the "balanced portfolio" concept—so that the public will see the advantages of alternative investments.

Our final question was broader, going beyond the specifics of this recent Pew survey to ask whether public opinion matters for policymakers more generally. If, then, the public responds in a well-rendered poll that they largely believe in a reformation of the nation's approaches to punishment, will we begin to see change as eager politicians respond to their constituents?

Cullen: A survey [like Pew's] can matter a great deal. Policymakers are not necessarily driven to act by public opinion surveys, but they are unlikely to pursue reforms if the public is seen as opposed. Policymakers generally overestimate the punitiveness of the public, [so this] is crucial in showing policymakers that they have considerable latitude in devising reasonable policies.

Jacobs: There is work in political science showing that the correlation between the attitudes of voters and congressional votes on policy issues varies by the policy. Most voters don't know anything about foreign policy, for instance, so there's no correlation. For economic policy, spending and things like that, there is a modest correlation. The only strong correlation you get between constituents' attitudes and how their congressional representative votes concerns moral issues, like civil rights, abortion, or capital punishment. So, I don't see [this survey] as consequential because public opinion doesn't affect most public policies much. There is little evidence that public opinion has a strong influence on complicated policies that aren't well publicized, such as a collection of laws that increase imprisonments or increase spending on corrections.

Travis: The question now is whether the public mood has turned, [if] the public now believes the prison budget can safely be reduced. [Pew's] survey results would suggest that this shift is possible. But it is too soon to know for certain. . . . So the question of the moment may be how best to capture the public mood—when the public is looking for a more balanced investment portfolio with reductions in prison budgets and increases in community supervision budgets—to map out a long-term strategy rather than seeking quick results through a program of early releases.

Garland: I [recently attended] a very powerful, inspiring social activist speech by Michelle Alexander . . . , the author of a book called *The New Jim Crow*, which . . . argues, I think powerfully (if unpersuasively) that . . . the system of mass confinement, which has been disproportionately suffered by black men (increasingly, by black women too), will not be undone by the kinds of legal reforms that are currently envisaged. It would take a social movement on the scale of the civil rights movement to undo it. And I think that she is right about that, but I think there's no prospect whatsoever of a social movement of that kind.

The punishment of criminal offenders is not an unpopular position, nor is it even a position that violates the values and the constitutional commitments of the American liberal, the American Democrat, or American civil liberties. It's a matter of scaling back excessive punishment, and I think that will only ever get done through the realization by legislators and by elites that rendering punishment questions as populist questions was a huge mistake. Because the answer will always be "More, please!" We're talking about what to do with violent offenders, dangerous offenders, but even drug offenders who might *one day* be violent and dangerous or who might be selling their drugs to "our children." The popular response, by and large, is "Lock them up. Let me not see them on my street, please." For that reason, it's very, very difficult to see a widespread social movement mobilized for and on behalf of criminal offenders.

That's a desperate reality, because the tragedy of American imprisonment can't be understated. It's been devastating for not just the men and women involved but for their communities, for their spouses, for their families, for their children, for their neighborhoods, and for the states in which they live.

PARTICIPANT PROFILES

Francis T. Cullen is in the departments of criminal justice and sociology at the University of Cincinnati. He is the author of *Rethinking Crime and Deviance Theory* (Rowman and Littlefield, 1987).

David Garland is in the departments of sociology and law at the New York University. He is the author of *Peculiar Institution: America's Death Penalty in an Age of Abolition* (Harvard University Press, 2010).

David Jacobs is in the department of sociology at The Ohio State University. He studies stratification and inequality, political sociology, and criminal justices.

Jeremy Travis is the president of John Jay College of Criminal Justice. He is the author of *But They All Come Back: Facing the Challenges of Prisoner Reentry* (Urban Institute Press, 2005).

a social welfare critique of contemporary crime control

RICHARD ROSENFELD AND STEVEN F. MESSNER

F ew politicians ever promise to *increase* crime rates, just as few constituents ever demand greater crime in their neighborhoods. But this anticrime consensus breaks down when we map out the different policy routes to reducing crime—and the sacrifices each might entail. A marginal drop in the crime rate would be cold comfort if it bankrupted the treasury or stripped citizens of their basic rights, yet such "big-picture" trade-offs are often obscured in the heat of a crime bill debate. As sociologists and criminologists, we use an "institutional perspective" to assess such questions about crime and its control. The value of an institutional perspective on crime is its explicit focus on the big picture: the overarching institutional structure of a society and the associated moral order. These macro-level phenomena shape the terrain within which individuals interact, and they generate the social pressures, incentives, and restraints (external and internal) that ultimately determine the prevailing pattern and level of crime in a society.

Assuming that the basic institutional arrangements of the developed nations are likely to be sustained for the foreseeable future, we can envision two basic policy approaches to crime: a criminal justice or security state approach and a social welfare approach. The first scenario entails lowering the crime rate by compensating within the criminal justice system for the less than desired performance of the socializing institutions of society, particularly the family and educational systems. Policy initiatives under this scenario are directed primarily toward restricting the *opportunities* for committing crime. The second scenario entails a broadening of the conceptualization of crime-control policy to encompass strategies for reducing criminal *motivations*, strategies that compensate for the weaknesses of a market economy in promoting and sustaining a viable moral order. We illustrate the first scenario by assessing the benefits and costs of mass incarceration and targeted ("hot spots") policing in the United States. We take up the second scenario in a discussion of the crime-control prospects of expansive social welfare policies.

reducing criminal opportunities through criminal justice

During the 1970s, several criminologists sought to explain the remarkable temporal stability in imprisonment rates in the United States and other nations. They referred to Emile Durkheim's idea that societies stabilize levels of punishment to maintain social solidarity. No sooner had the "stability of punishment" hypothesis been advanced, than prison populations in the United States began climbing to historically unprecedented levels. Imprisonment rates increased fivefold from the mid-1970s to 2010. So much for stability.

A classic statement in the sociology of punishment links the size of the prison population to changes in the labor market. According to this argument, prisons help regulate the supply of labor in capitalist societies. When labor is in short supply and unemployment rates are low, pressures mount to reduce the size of the prison population. When labor markets are slack and unemployment rises, the prison population expands. Research on the labor supply hypothesis has returned mixed results, at best. And how can it account for the era of mass incarceration in the United States, when imprisonment rates quintupled with no apparent connection to oscillating unemployment during the same period?

Interpreted broadly, however, the labor supply argument does help to explain the historical relationship between punishment policy and the political economy of the United States. It also illustrates how we typically rely on the criminal justice system to compensate for deficiencies elsewhere in the institutional order. As the economy has undergone structural change, from the rise of the factory system in the nineteenth century to the decline in the demand for unskilled factory labor in the latter part of the twentieth century, the policy and practice of "corrections," as it is still quaintly called, have adapted. Mass incarceration arose, in part, as a response to the concomitant expansion of the urban underclass in the 1970s and '80s. Chronically high levels of joblessness in American inner cities, growing family disruption, and community disorder and decline prompted policymakers to search for substitute means of social control. "In a very real sense," sociologist Elliott Currie wrote (on page 46 of *Reaping What We Sow*), "our swollen prison system has functioned as a costly and ineffective alternative to serious efforts to address those enduring social deficits."

Mass incarceration *is* very costly, but is it ineffective? To understand the impact of imprisonment on crime, it is useful to invoke criminologists' distinction between *criminal motivations* and *criminal opportunities*. Criminal motivations refer to the desire or propensity of individuals to engage in

crime and the punished

criminal behavior. Criminal opportunities are situational inducements (an unlocked door, an open window, lack of surveillance) and impediments (locks, barriers, guards) that make crime more or less easy to commit. Persons with little or no criminal motivation are unlikely to commit crime regardless of the opportunity to do so. But even highly motivated would-be offenders may refrain from criminal behavior if there aren't adequate criminal opportunities. In other words, for criminality to give rise to criminal acts, there must be some opportunity to commit crime. Imprisonment is a potent method for suppressing criminal acts by denying incarcerated offenders the opportunity to commit crimes (at least, against the general public).

It is quite reasonable to expect that policies that task the criminal justice system with compensating for poor institutional performance elsewhere would exact a high price in economic, political, and social capital. The United States is a rich nation and can afford to maintain a huge corrections complex, even though mounting corrections expenditures have far outstripped the overall growth in the U.S. economy. But corrections costs are borne primarily by state and local governments, and they have grown at roughly double the rate of state and local outlays for education, health care, and policing over the past 30 years. Each additional dollar spent on prisons, jails, and community corrections is a dollar that states and local areas cannot devote to other pressing needs. Those needs include improvements in education and early childhood interventions that hold some promise for reducing criminal motivations.

As costly as mass incarceration in the United States is in purely economic terms, it also has significant political and social costs. Researchers have only recently begun to analyze them in depth, but they include imprisonment's destabilizing effects on families and communities, the growing population of permanently disenfranchised ex-prisoners and other convicted felons, and, quite possibly, higher crime rates over the long run. Moreover, the costs of mass incarceration are not spread evenly across the population; they are borne disproportionately by African Americans. Arrest rates for many serious offenses are higher among African Americans than other groups, but only a small part of the growth in incarceration over the past three decades has resulted from a rise in crime. Most of the growth is from changes in sentencing and recommitment policies that are more likely to affect the life chances of African Americans.

It should be apparent that simply adding up the economic losses from crime (medical expenses, time lost from work, etc.) and comparing them with the economic costs of imprisonment does not capture the full range of costs associated with either. Nor is it clear how economists' efforts to fully monetize the costs of crime (i.e., to assign a dollar value to all costs, no matter how intangible) can help policymakers and informed citizens make the difficult political and moral trade-offs inherent in deciding how many people to lock up to lower the crime rate.

So, the costs of mass incarceration are high, difficult to control, difficult to measure, and unequally distributed across the population. It is natural to ask whether the costs of any policy equal or exceed the benefits. This question proves very difficult to answer in the case of mass incarceration. For one thing, the magnitude and duration of the effects of imprisonment growth on crime remain uncertain. But more importantly, it is far from clear how we should weigh the benefits of less crime against the escalating costs of mass incarceration. How much are we willing to increase community instability or voter disenfranchisement to avert one additional robbery or burglary (or 10 or 100) through increased incarceration? How much less should we spend on education or health care to avert an additional homicide? The costs and (possible) benefits of mass incarceration simply do not share a common metric against which such trade-offs can be reconciled.

It is instructive to consider whether many of the purported benefits of mass incarceration can be attained through alternative means. Can we achieve whatever crime reductions are attributable to mass incarceration by instead implementing programs and policies that are less costly to the public purse, affected families and communities (of both offenders and victims), and a democratic polity? Crime policy analysts Steven Durlauf and Daniel Nagin maintain that both imprisonment and crime can be reduced by transferring resources currently devoted to prisons to expanding policing strategies of proven effectiveness. Despite the obstacles associated with moving budget expenditures from one level of government to another, in principle, there is much to recommend such a policy shift. Carefully targeting enforcement strategies to crime "hot spots" has been shown to reduce crime without merely displacing it to other areas. Like incarceration, though, targeted policing simply reduces criminal opportunities.

Criminal opportunities, in our view, are best thought of as *proximate* causes of crime, characteristics of the immediate situation or milieu that trigger or restrain criminal acts. Criminal opportunities are, by their very nature, ephemeral and subject to situational variation; that's one reason they're more amenable to policy manipulation, such as the move to targeted patrols and other forms of "smart policing." But measures directed solely at manipulating criminal opportunities fail to address the *moral* sources of crime. That does not make crime prevention through opportunity reduction ineffective, at least in the short run, but it does raise questions about its limits and costs.

One important cost involves the scope and penetration of social control entailed in eliminating opportunities for crime. Opportunity reduction often involves restrictions on freedom of movement and other everyday liberties (as anyone who has traveled by air over the past decade can attest). Young minority males who are routinely stopped and questioned by the police pay an especially high price for the benefits of at least some versions of targeted policing. Omnipresent barriers, gates, grates, alarms, cameras, screening and tracking technologies, and security personnel represent the extension of the disciplinary principles and devices of the prison to public life. Policies and practices that reduce opportunities for crime must be part of any comprehensive program of crime control. But they cannot be the *only* means by which policymakers try to maintain order. For those who prize democratic values and are mindful of the collateral costs of crime-control efforts, this is an important point. By implementing ever more extensive and intrusive controls, a society can likely reduce criminal opportunities even further. But do we really want to live in such a world of sanitized surveillance? There are other ways to control crime that impose fewer collateral costs. Ameliorating the deep-seated structural and cultural sources of criminal motivation may actually prove less invasive to *all* citizens than seeking to eliminate criminal opportunities through a thousand cuts to individual freedoms and democratic values.

reducing criminal motivations through social welfare policy

If criminal opportunities are *proximate* causes of crime, criminal motivations and the conditions that stimulate them are closer to *ultimate* causes: they reside deeper in the social structure and are implicated in a society's basic institutional patterns. For example, when a class of citizens is subject to grinding poverty, inequality, and inhumane treatment—as is often the case in totalitarian regimes—criminal motivations may rise, even in the absence of criminal opportunities.

Broadly understood, crime-control policy must also seek to replenish the moral bases of social order and criminal justice. This will require structural changes that enhance the regulatory capacities of social institutions (such as the strong families and communities that play a central role in determining the crime rate). We believe the most effective and realistic way of producing enduring crime reductions in the developed nations is to reduce the dependence of populations on the performance of the market economy.

It seems likely that the contemporary structure of developed nations' market economies will remain highly resistant to fundamental change, but market forces need not dominate other social institutions, especially to the degree they do in the United States. The institutional balance of power varies markedly across the developed capitalist societies, and the modern welfare state is a potent counterweight to the market in most of them. The welfare state is part of what economic historian Karl Polanyi called the great "double movement" in the development of modern capitalism; it has prevented the market economy from completely remaking other institutions in its own image. And several studies show that societies in which extensive social welfare policies shield the most vulnerable members of the population from the full brunt of market forces tend to experience lower levels of serious criminal violence than those with less generous and more restrictive policies. The U.S. homicide rate of 4.8 per 100,000, for example, is four to five times that of social democratic welfare states such as Sweden, Norway, Denmark, and the Netherlands.

The promise of the welfare state for crime control is not simply to compensate for the deficiencies of the market economy by providing for the unmet material needs of a population (i.e., giving people what they need so that they won't steal it). Social welfare programs, according to political scientist

Bo Rothstein (on page 2 of *Just Institutions Matter*), "are not just instrumental arrangements; they are also, and in a high degree, expressions of definite moral conceptions." The morality of the modern welfare state emphasizes equality, fairness, justice, and solidarity. As such, the welfare state would seem the ideal social housing for protection against the material *and* moral failings of the market economy.

If this description of the welfare state strikes the reader as curious, it's because today's welfare state has come under attack from, it seems, all sides. Political liberals question the capacity of governments to provide extensive social insurance for citizens in an era of heightened global competition for capital, resources, and markets. Some social observers worry that the welfare state erodes voluntary sources of mutual aid and civic engagement. But the harshest attack comes from the political Right, and it goes directly to the moral foundations of the welfare state. From this perspective, the welfare state is inherently unjust because it forcibly transfers wealth from producers to the undeserving; it saps individual initiative by creating a culture of dependency; and it causes more, not less, crime. By the end of the twentieth century, the modern welfare state was on the ideological defensive against such harsh accusations.

Even if we were to grant such criticisms, however, any welfare state intrusions on individual rights and liberties must be weighed against the real and expanding intrusions of our current criminal justice approach to reducing criminal opportunities. When cast in this light, welfare state policies to reduce criminal motivation appear more benign than "security state" policies to restrict criminal opportunities. As we have argued, simply manipulating criminal opportunities cannot, by itself, generate sizeable and sustained crime reductions. Further, this approach poses risks to individual freedom and other cherished values. The pursuit of a collectively tolerable crime rate instead requires an approach to crime control that is keenly sensitive to the larger institutional dynamics of society.

At present, in the immediate aftermath of the most severe recession since the Great Depression, when many developed nations face the prospect of huge cutbacks in government spending, defense of the welfare state assumes a special urgency. We see no better way to limit crime and promote justice in contemporary developed societies than to rein in the excesses of market economies with policies that guarantee a decent standard of living to all citizens and, by their very nature, reinforce a sense of mutual obligation and collective responsibility. That is the historic promise of the welfare state as part of a vital and responsive democratic polity. No other institution on the world stage today is as likely to limit crime and promote justice without sacrificing individual liberties and democratic values.

RECOMMENDED READING

Elliott Currie. 2012. "Reaping What We Sow: The Impact of Economic Justice on Criminal Justice," in *To Build a Better Criminal Justice System: 25 Experts Envision the Next 25 Years of Reform*, Washington, DC: The Sentencing Project. A compelling argument for combating crime with policies that reduce poverty and inequality.

Steven N. Durlauf and Daniel S. Nagin. 2011. "Imprisonment and Crime: Can Both Be Reduced?" *Criminology & Public Policy* 10(1):13–54. Maintains that both imprisonment and crime can be reduced by transferring resources from the prison system to "hot spots" policing.

Steven F. Messner, Richard Rosenfeld, and Susanne Karstedt. 2013. "Social Institutions and Crime," in Francis T. Cullen and Pamela Wilcox (editors), *Oxford Handbook of Criminological Theory*, New York: Oxford University Press. Develops an "institutional perspective" on crime that links crime rates to the structure, legitimacy, and performance of social institutions.

Karl Polanyi. 2001 (1944). *The Great Transformation: The Political and Economic Origins of Our Time*, Boston: Beacon Press. A classic statement in defense of strong social welfare policies to protect populations from the material and moral failings of capitalism.

Richard Rosenfeld and Steven F. Messner. 2010. "The Normal Crime Rate, the Economy, and Mass Incarceration: An Institutional-

Anomie Perspective on Crime-Control Policy," in Hugh D. Barlow and Scott H. Decker (editors), *Criminology and Public Policy: Putting Theory to Work*. Philadelphia: Temple University Press. Proposes that high imprisonment rates are the price American society pays for the normal functioning of its economic and social institutions.

Bo Rothstein. 1998. *Just Institutions Matter: The Moral and Political Logic of the Universal Welfare State*, Cambridge, UK: Cambridge University Press. Uses Sweden as the primary example to defend the modern welfare state against several contemporary criticisms.

12

juvenile lifers, learning to lead

MICHELLE INDERBITZIN, TREVOR WALRAVEN, AND JOSHUA CAIN

t is quite extraordinary to sit in a Lifers Club meeting at the Oregon State Penitentiary. First, the facts: Individuals who identify as "lifers" have been convicted of taking a life and have made a commitment to change their own. Only about 5% of the prison's population is among its members, and they generally face decades together in this insular society of captives. As might be expected, looking around the room, there are older men, grizzled and withered from years of confinement; hard-to-miss tattoos proclaiming past loyalties, lost loves, and diminished hope; and cynicism in the eyes of those who think their fall was harder or less just than was warranted. And then, against every prison stereotype, there are the young elected officers of the club, working the room with focus and patience. These leaders listen to others' concerns, accept advice and suggestions, and steer the Lifers

Club toward positive contributions to the "inside" and "outside" community.

The men in the room (including two of this article's authors) have made a choice to be active members of the Lifers Club; in doing so, they recognize the harsh reality that the terrible acts of their pasts can never be erased or undone. They hope to use the long years in prison to come to terms with their histories and prepare for very different futures. The ledgers may never balance, but the club's young officers share a deep belief that the lifers owe a significant debt to society. They are focused on beginning reparations. The positive energy is palpable: If it were not for the "prison blues" (standard-issue denim), the stark setting, and the uniformed officers standing in the corners, it would be easy to mistake this group of young men as graduate students, businessmen, or fraternity alumni. They are clean cut, active, and vital. But they live within the walls of a maximum-security prison.

Trevor, the current president of the Lifers Club, is all laser focus and determination, striving to meet his proclaimed goal to give 100% of his effort 100% of the time. At the age of 14, Trevor's time started on a life sentence with 30 years served before the possibility of parole. Not yet 29, Trevor has now spent just over half of his life behind bars. In one way, Trevor is fortunate: because he was too young at 14 to be sentenced under the state's mandatory minimum sentencing laws, he will soon have the opportunity to get a "second look." His sentence and conduct will be reviewed; if he is not released at that time, he will be entitled to regular hearings with the parole board.

Trevor and the other elected Lifers Club leaders are strikingly young. Four of the five officers were teenagers at the time of the crimes that brought them to prison. The vice president, James, is a poet and self-taught artist. His goal is to have a family when he gets out of prison. James was 16 when he and his friends made the worst mistake of their lives; his first offense brought him a mandatory-minimum sentence of 25 years. He is midway through that sentence now, a young man in his early thirties trying to grow, mature, and find meaning while serving another full decade in prison. Trevor's older brother, Joshua, is the secretary of the Lifers Club; Josh was 18 at the time of the crime that brought him and his brother to prison. In his early thirties now, he too is serving a 25-year mandatory-minimum sentence. Blessed with extra doses of charisma, Josh is focused on self-improvement, balancing college classes, work, and family responsibilities from within the prison. Fred, another young leader in the Lifers Club, has a distinctive voice and humor. He has worked to overcome his troubled youth to become a positive role model for the son he left on the outside.

Most of the young officers of the Lifers Club are in prison as first-time offenders (albeit for very serious crimes), and they have quite literally grown up in prison. Each was incarcerated in his teens, but will likely have the opportunity to get out of prison after serving long mandatory-minimum sentences. If and when they are released, they will be middle-aged or older, facing entirely new challenges and a vastly changed culture outside the prison walls. In the meantime, they must decide how to channel their youth and vitality behind bars. The long lists of activities and accomplishments these lifers have chosen demonstrate that prison time does not have to be wasted time. They believe they can be instruments of positive change within the prison while also finding ways to contribute to the society outside.

Scanning a club meeting, one can count several other lifers who were 15 or 16 years old at the time of their crimes. Many were convicted while still teenagers. While official sentences of life without parole are rare, some members of the Lifers Club will face what criminologists Robert Johnson and Sandra McGunigall-Smith have called a "virtual death sentence"—a slow death by incarceration rather than execution. In some cases, judges have sentenced juveniles to longer than their life expectancy (for example, 15-year-old school shooter Kip Kinkel received a sentence of 110 years without the possibility of parole), but in most cases, the juvenile lifers must serve a minimum number of years before appearing before the parole board. The parole board then has the discretion to release or continue holding the prisoner indefinitely. Because these are often highly publicized homicide cases, it is frequently politically untenable for the parole board to opt for release.

teenage lifers

When people under the age of 18 are sentenced to long prison stints, they frequently start their confinement in juvenile or youth correctional facilities. Generally, these facilities have a smaller staff-inmate ratio and more focus on education and rehabilitation. This consideration of placement implicitly recognizes the difference between teen and adult maturity levels. Yet, under mandatory-minimum sentencing, enacted amid widespread fear of a new generation of juvenile "super-predators" in the 1990s, teens are frequently given sentence lengths as long as their adult counterparts. More troubling, the latest neuroscientific evidence shows convincingly that adolescents' brains are still in formation; sentences went up in the '90s, but the most current science says teenagers may actually be less mature and capable of making good decisions than was previously believed. As psychologist Laurence Steinberg has shown, adolescents tend to be more impulsive, more susceptible to peer influence, less oriented to the future, and less capable of weighing the costs and benefits of actions than adults.

This research on the adolescent brain may—and should—cause us to rethink our punitive treatment and sentencing of juvenile offenders. As Steinberg notes, if we recognize the difference in adolescent development and brain function, juvenile offenders should be treated more leniently than adults. In recent years, the Supreme Court has made policy separating juveniles from adult offenders in terms of the most serious sanctions, ruling that juvenile offenders can no longer be sentenced to death (*Roper v. Simmons*, 2005) or to life without parole (*Graham v. Florida*, 2010; *Miller v. Alabama*, 2012). The 2012 Court was deeply divided in issuing the ruling that sentencing youth to die in prison is cruel and unusual punishment, and while this decision offers some hope to the approximately two thousand adolescents serving life without parole in the United States, many thousands more are routinely given sentences that send them to prison for decades.

Whether it is ethical to hold teenagers fully responsible for their criminal acts when they do not enjoy the other rights and privileges of adulthood is a question for continuing and vigorous debate. In the meantime, those committed to life sentences as juveniles must survive twenty to thirty years in prison with their sanity intact. Some may spend years in anger and rebellion, but eventually each must decide how he or she wants to spend the years, whether to simply "do the time" or instead become a "gleaner," as convict-criminologist John Irwin described those who seek productive outlets to improve their skills and minds in the prison environment. They may channel their energy into education, programs, and prison clubs, or they may become self-taught artists, learning guitar, drawing, painting, or craftsmanship working with leather or jewelry. As the young leaders of the Lifers Club demonstrate, individuals are capable of exercising efficacy and choice even in desolate circumstances.

growing into leadership

For many teenagers charged with serious crimes, their first transition to imprisonment occurs in county jail or detention as they await trial. As Josh explains, "I grew up a lot in county jail, because I was there for almost a full year before heading to prison. I was 18 when I got arrested, and so it was quite a shock being locked up for the first time. I looked even younger than 18, and the jailers didn't really know what to do with me at first, so they kept me in solitary confinement for the first 2 weeks. . . . Awaiting trial is a scary time, and I just kept thinking that I couldn't possibly get convicted and there was no way I would be sentenced to 25 years. But then I kept watching my fellow prisoners getting convicted and sent to prison, and I had no clue about the real justice system or the way things worked." Once he was transferred to prison, Josh remembers feeling lonely, intimidated, anxious, scared, and sad. He was afraid to let his guard down, a fear that has had long-term impact: "I was a 135-lb. boy at 18. I put on 50 pounds the first year because, in prison, size equals strength. . . . I built up a pretty tough shell, a weird kind of filter, something I still struggle with."

Perhaps surprisingly, Trevor found being one of the youngest men in prison a comfort: "Strangely enough, it has been more uncomfortable to grow 'old' in prison (relative as it may be) . . . there's always been older prisoners looking out for my best interest and an amazing support system from my family. Having my brother [Josh] serving time with me . . . is very sad, [but] in other ways it certainly has its benefits. Knowing without any doubt that I have someone I can count on is of great value." An experience when he was first incarcerated at 14 had a positive impact on Trevor: "The very first detention center I was housed at after losing my freedom had a teacher that had the words: 'Patience, Endurance & Self-control' written all over the classroom. These words have also been huge motivators to guide my life—a pretty positive message for the first months of my incarceration. I've also developed an understanding that, no matter where I live, ultimately I make the decisions that direct my future. We all have the power of choice, even if only in how we react to the actions of others."

Aging in prison is inevitable. Growth is optional. Those entering correctional institutions and immersed in prison culture as teenagers face an especially difficult path in their attempts to mature and develop into the men they hope to become, men their families can be proud of. Josh quickly figured out that he wanted to make his time in prison as productive as possible. He pursued self-improvement whenever he had the opportunity: "I took cognitive skills classes when I felt a need to be better at dealing with my thoughts and feelings. I took jobs that would teach me a skill I wanted. I took parenting classes because I wanted to be a better parent (and a better son)." His relationships with both his brother on the inside and his family on the outside help him to "keep my focus on freedom and real world problems instead of becoming institutionalized and concerning myself only with the dramas of prison. Having a relationship with my wife and the children she brings to our marriage has helped me to grow and mature in ways I doubt I would have without her."

Following his older brother's lead, Trevor, too, has sought out opportunities to develop skills and become a responsible adult within the prison system, but he recognizes the challenges of doing so in such a restrictive setting: "I really didn't have 'responsibilities' of an adult before I lost my freedom. Even today, while I do my best to acquire those kinds of responsibilities, until given the opportunity in the free world, I'll not truly know what it is to be an adult who's responsible for their own welfare."

While he cannot test whether he is ready for adult responsibilities in the larger society, Trevor focused on earning his high school diploma while in a youth correctional facility and then shifted his focus to employment and job skills as a young adult in prison. He put in long hours in the prison's industrial maintenance shop, learning and growing into a leadership role. His recent involvement in college classes and a brief stint as a clerk for the Lifers Club shifted his energy and focus, and his trajectory into program and club leadership has been swift. Trevor became treasurer of the Lifers Club and was quickly elected president, the youngest ever chosen to represent the membership. He takes the Lifers Unlimited Club's mission statement—to "improve the quality of life for those inside and outside of these walls"—seriously and utilizes the patience and persistence he has cultivated to make positive changes in his environment.

In viewing their roles as leaders in the Lifers Club, both Trevor and Josh are quick to point out the importance of respect and mentoring. In recounting his transition into prison, Josh explains: "I just tried to conduct myself respectably and I was lucky to have the other guys around me who were patient enough to correct me if I crossed the line and talk to me about any social mistakes I made in my new society...[they] gave me the tools I needed to survive...I still receive advice and help from my peers." Trevor learned from his older brother and prison elders, heeding advice such as "Give your word sparingly and adhere to it like iron. Be polite and appreciative and expect the same in return." His prison socialization undoubtedly helped propel Trevor into his leadership role with the Lifers Club: "The 'old timers' appreciate seeing someone so young who knows what respect is, knows how to do time, and has the values and morals that seem to be missing from many youth who cycle in and out of these prisons and institutions now days."

hope and second chances

Hope is a precious commodity in prison. Trevor says that even people in dark circumstance are capable of change: "Prisoners are still human beings. We do owe a debt to society and, regardless of whether or not we can ever pay that debt, we are most definitely able to change at any point along the way. Hope is something that everyone needs: Give second chances, provide the tools for people to grow but don't force them to grow."

Second chances have been increasingly difficult to come by for adolescent offenders since the 1980s. Public opinion studies by criminologist Brandon Applegate and colleagues show that Americans generally support rehabilitation and a "tough love" approach for serious juvenile offenders. Unfortunately, the public's apparent support for rehabilitative treatment has yet to significantly influence legislation; in policy circles, juvenile offenders are currently offered little love at all. As Alex Piquero and colleagues have noted, "support for a social welfare-oriented juvenile justice system is widespread, persistent, and deeply entrenched. Yet, despite this unwavering public opinion, punitive policies continue to be enacted."

Young men who have come of age in prison can offer tremendous insight into what it means to grow up behind bars. While we have focused here on the experience of just two brothers, they represent a far larger brotherhood of those convicted of serious crimes as teenagers and sentenced to spend decades in prison. Both Trevor and Josh are troubled by inflexible mandatory-minimum sentencing and believe there should be more discretion in the justice system. It's not necessarily an argument for lenience; instead, they see a clear need for careful consideration of individual circumstances and cases. Trevor explains: "I don't believe that I should have received a sentence of 'life in prison with a minimum

30 years served before the possibility of parole'; however, I also don't believe I should have been released at the age of 21 or 25. I think that regular consideration should be given to evaluate how a person has grown and changed, as well as consideration regarding the safety and security of the community."

Josh advocates an alternative philosophy of punishment and justice, but ends with a more modest recommendation: "[E]very case, situation, and person is different and should be treated accordingly. Sentencing should be about restorative justice, understanding the damage done and working to correct it, while at the same time correcting the behavior that caused it . . . punishment is commonly not corrective, as recidivism rates show. Prison is frequently a school on criminal behaviors, and those who are young and impressionable are even more susceptible to making those poor choices that will likely lead them to future crime, quite possibly worse than their current offense. I believe that age should be a strong mitigating factor in the sentencing process."

These two men, who came to prison as boys, have grown into roles as young leaders of a maximum-security prison's most stable inmate organization, the Lifers Unlimited Club. They are finding and channeling the energy to change not only their own lives but also the actions and culture of the Club and the whole prison. They do what they can to prepare for their chance to get out and build lives in the community;

as Josh put it: "[W]e serve ourselves best by using the time to better ourselves and become better people and better prepared for success in freedom." In the intervening years, however, there are issues they care about deeply within the prison, and they will work to find compromises and resolutions. They make the best of a bad situation and find meaning in their lives, even as they hope for a day they can leave prison walls behind forever.

RECOMMENDED READING

Brandon K. Applegate, Robin King Davis, and Francis T. Cullen. 2009. "Reconsidering Child Saving: The Extent and Correlates of Public Support for Excluding Youths from the Juvenile Court," *Crime & Delinquency* 55(1):51–77. Results from a public opinion poll on juvenile offenders and appropriate sentencing.

John Irwin. 2009. *Lifers: Seeking Redemption in Prison.* New York: Routledge. Ethnography of prisoners who have served more than 20 years in prison.

Robert Johnson and Sandra McGunigall-Smith. 2008. "Life without Parole, America's Other Death Penalty: Notes on Life under Sentence of Death by Incarceration," *The Prison Journal* 88(2):328–346. Uses original interviews with prisoners to explore the sentence and experience of life without parole.

Alex R. Piquero, Francis T. Cullen, James D. Unnever, Nicole L. Piquero, and Jill A. Gordon. 2010. "Never Too Late: Public Optimism about Juvenile Rehabilitation," *Punishment & Society* 12(2):187–207. Examines preferences for public policy associated with juvenile crime.

Laurence Steinberg. 2009. "Adolescent Development and Juvenile Justice," *Annual Review of Clinical Psychology* 27(3):307–326. Summarizes findings on brain, cognitive, and social development in adolescence and discusses implications for juvenile offenders.

discovering desistance, with shadd maruna and fergus mcneill

SARAH SHANNON AND SARAH LAGESON

S hadd Maruna and Fergus McNeill have spent the better part of their careers asking questions about "desistance": *why* and *how* people transition out of crime. As their work has shown, desistance is a tricky concept to define and measure. While some think of it as a permanent cessation of criminal behavior over several years, others use a more fluid definition that accepts that episodes of re-offending may occur. Either way, desistance is a positive outcome for individuals and for society as a whole, as it involves long-term abstinence from crime among those with a history of serious criminal behavior.

In their latest project, the two scholars—along with Steve Farrall (at the University of Sheffield) and Claire Lightowler (of the Institute for Research and Innovation in Social

Services)—collaborated with former prisoners to tell the story of desistance *with* those who are actively engaging in the process. Their documentary film, *The Road from Crime*, is a "co-production" with Allan Weaver, a Scottish "ex-offender" turned probation officer (and author of the book *So You Think You Know Me?*) documenting his journey to understand his own process of desistance and those of others like him. In merging social science research insights with firsthand experience, the collaboration delivers a fresh perspective on desistance through film. The documentary was produced as part of the larger Discovering Desistance project, which aims to share knowledge and improve understanding of why people desist from crime.

In a podcast interview with TSP's Sarah Lageson, Maruna and McNeill talked about why they went from writing books and articles about desistance to making films.

Maruna: The academic lecture is a classic, it's what keeps us in business at some level, but it's not necessarily the best way to convey information (think how many lectures we've all slept through in the past!). We thought bringing the subject a bit to life, as you can do on film, would be a better strategy at some level. Film can put a human face on desistence (in this case, several faces come out). It brings something important that books and the articles can't—when you can look into somebody's eyes and see them as a fellow human.

This chapter is also something of a co-production. In addition to speaking with these experts, we dug deeply into their academic writings and materials specially created for the film. To faithfully present this vision of desistance, we draw directly from each of these sources, as well as our interview with Maruna and McNeill. For example, both Weaver's journey and the goals of the collaboration are introduced on the film's Web site, blogs.iriss.org.uk/discoveringdesistance:

In our documentary, *The Road from Crime*, Allan Weaver asks a simple question: What can we learn from those former prisoners who have successfully "desisted" from criminal behavior or "gone straight?" Starting where it all began for him on the streets of his hometown and in Barlinnie Prison in Glasgow, Allan sets off to understand how individuals like himself get caught up in cycles of crime and punishment, and how they break out of these patterns and move on to new lives. This journey takes him across the UK, meeting an array of ex-prisoners and ex-prisoner activist groups, probation leaders, and criminological experts from London to Washington, D.C.

One of the biggest hurdles for former prisoners is what sociologist Erving Goffman called "stigma"—overcoming the simple fact of *being* a former prisoner. Following Weaver's journey, the vicious cycle becomes clear: Crime leads to contact with the criminal justice system, which can result in even more crime through labeling and stigmatization. Criminologists have focused so much on the problem of "recidivism" or returning to crime, however, that the success stories of desistance remain largely untold. As *The Road from Crime* Web site puts it:

> The exit at the prison gate often appears to be a revolving door with nearly 60 percent of released prisoners reoffending within two years of their release. Prisons and probation departments have, almost literally, tried everything in efforts to rehabilitate offenders over the past century, but the results have been uniformly bleak, leading many to conclude that "nothing works." In the past ten years, however, a group of criminologists have hit upon what should have been an obvious source of inspiration for prisoner rehabilitation: the other 40%!

The upsurge of interest in the other 40%—from scholars, practitioners, and policymakers around the world—is partly driven by budget concerns and the high costs of criminal punishment. If the criminal justice system could more effectively hasten the transition from offender to *former* offender, there is much to be gained. We would not only save the money it would cost to reincarcerate repeat offenders but we would also reap the benefits of their productive contributions—in the taxes they pay, the families they support, and the positive roles they could play in their communities.

Every desistance story is different, but most tend to involve both external support from others and internal change and self-discovery. The film shows ex-prisoners speaking directly about the people who believed in them when others had lost hope and about rediscovering their self-worth—realizing that they too had something to offer others, especially, for many, their own children.

defining desistance

Countless studies have asked what causes people to start committing crime, but far fewer have asked why people *stop*. Reading the paper "How and Why People Stop Offending: Discovering Desistance" by McNeill, Lightowler, Farrall, and Maruna, we learn that the "age-crime" curve is one of the few near certainties in criminal justice. For most people, crime peaks in the teenage years, and then declines quickly thereafter. But why and how they desist is not well known, even though it is one of the key outcomes that the criminal justice system is supposed to achieve.

Early desistance theories from criminologists like Sheldon and Eleanor Glueck focused on "maturational reform"—a natural process linked to aging. Although age is one of the best predictors of desistance, aging involves a great range of processes, including biological changes, social transitions, and life experiences. For age to be a meaningful explanation of desistance, we need to ask what it is about aging that makes a difference.

For the past two decades, sociologist Robert Sampson and John Laub, former director of the National Institute of Justice, theorized that committing crime is more likely when the bond between an individual and society is weakened or broken. They argue that at various points of the life course, formal and informal social institutions help to solidify the bond between the individual and society and reduce criminal behavior. For adolescents, schools, families, and peer groups influence the bond between young people and the broader community. For adults, employment, marriage, and parenthood operate in a similar way. Key events or "turning points" (like a new job opportunity) can trigger changes in an individual's bond to society and influence crime and desistance patterns.

Sampson and Laub's work has been dominant since the 1990s, though it has been challenged by criminologists like

Michael Gottfredson and Travis Hirschi. They contend that life events like marriage and employment are themselves governed by a trait they call self-control, which crystallizes in early childhood. Psychologist Terrie Moffitt argues that there are really two types of criminal offenders. The first are "adolescence-limited" who start to offend in early adolescence and cease offending relatively soon afterward. The second are "life-course persistent," who start much earlier and continue to commit crime well past their teenage years.

These latter approaches perhaps don't seem to leave much room for interventions that would hasten desistance among those with "low self-control" or "life-course persistent" offending patterns. Maruna and McNeill are more optimistic, emphasizing the importance of self-concept and identity—as well as of social support. Maruna has found that to desist from crime, people need to develop "a coherent, prosocial identity for themselves." This happens when they see themselves in control of their futures and have a clear sense of purpose and meaning in their lives. Desisters also find a way to make sense of their past lives and find some redeeming value in the time spent in the criminal justice system. The ex-prisoners Maruna interviewed often said they wanted to put these experiences "to good use" by helping young people in similar circumstances to their own avoid the mistakes they had made. Sociologists Peggy Giordano and colleagues describe a similar process in their four-part "theory of cognitive transformation" where they argue that the desistance process involves a "general cognitive openness to change," exposure and reaction to "hooks for change" or turning points, envisioning an appealing and conventional "replacement self," and a transformation in how deviant behavior is viewed.

Maruna and Thomas LeBel, in their chapter "The Desistance Paradigm in Correctional Practice: From Programs to Lives," also see an important role for "delabelling," in which positive behavior change is recognized by others and reflected back to the desister. They argue that people start to believe that they can successfully change their lives when those around them demonstrate that they also believe change is possible. Put another way, not only must a person accept conventional society to go straight but conventional society must recognize and accept that this person has changed as well.

The researchers point out that focusing on desistance from crime moves us away from ideas of people as "offenders," "criminals," or "prisoners" and encourages us to think about how these statuses change over time. In fact, today's "young offender" is more likely to become tomorrow's "new father" than tomorrow's "habitual criminal." This means valuing people for who they are and for what they could become, rather than judging them for what they have done. To really improve criminal justice efforts to help people desist from crime and find their way to reintegration, we'll need insights from desisters like Weaver as well as social scientists.

filming desistance

We asked Maruna and McNeill how they got involved in making *The Road From Crime* and why they wanted to tell the desistance story in film.

What's different about telling a research story in a film, rather than in other media?

Maruna: We found out there are many parallels between the way we do research and the way documentary experts make films. If you think about all the difficulties of doing qualitative research, you've got to magnify them by 10 or 20 fold when you add the cameras and so forth. We always have technological glitches when you're doing interviews—your digital recorder won't work or you've run out of battery or these things—well, when you've got the sound boom, the camera, the lights, something always is going wrong! The easiest interview turned into an hour and a half, two hours in the field because of those technology problems with film.

McNeill: We wrote the voiceover together . . . several times and gave it to the director. And the director wrote back to us and said . . . and this is paraphrasing, "Why don't you trust my film?" And the . . . obvious message was that in documentary filmmaking, you leave some of the responsibility, obviously, with the viewer to interpret what they're seeing.

Are there different practical and ethical issues involved in making this sort of film?

Maruna: There are important ethical issues in qualitative research. It's crucial to be able to protect people's identities and to not expose people to risks of harm. All of that is magnified when you're shining a camera at somebody and projecting their image online. The awkwardness of the interview becomes a lot more difficult when there are so many people involved, rather than just you and a tape recorder. But in terms of the actual process, it involves interviewing people, getting their narratives, and then the editing, which is really where all the hard work is. It was essentially doing an inductive analysis, just like for an academic article or a book.

How did making the film unearth new research ideas?

Maruna: Almost all of the major themes in the film can be found in *Making Good* or any of Fergus's articles on the topic, but making the film did put some of those themes in a sharper focus. For example, the "contagion effect" of desistance, where two of the interviewees in Washington, D.C., are talking about "I went straight because he went straight and I could see that was a road for me." We heard that theme a number of other times from others, and in the research, but they came to life in the film.

McNeill: The approach that we took in the project overall was essentially one of co-production—so, we bring a certain kind of knowledge to the process, but we respect and value and want to enter into a dialogue with other forms of knowledge (the knowledge of ex-offenders, the knowledge of family members and supporters, the knowledge of practitioners, of policymakers, and the knowledge of the artists, the creative artists involved in the filmmaking process). The whole ethos of the thing is to try to co-construct a narrative that has meaning and validity and some kind of truth amongst all of those parties. That's what generates the kind of unique quality of the project's outcomes. They are not just an academic reading of a social problem, delivered back to people in the field, people affected by the problem in question, they are something that we produced together.

The idea of co-producing knowledge is close to the heart of The Society Pages project, but can co-production really help develop effective policies to reduce crime among released prisoners?

McNeill: One major finding out of the project was not a substantive recommendation for criminal justice in any specific domain but rather the idea that, if we want people to engage with justice processes in order that they might, in some way transform their lives and be supported towards integration in society, then it's absurd to imagine that we can do that other than co-productively—other than by engaging with them, respecting them, their knowledge, their expertise, their lived experience. People are working hard at trying to change and address their problems, but if people in the community aren't going to accept them back, then all that hard work is liable to be in vain.

PARTICIPANT PROFILES

Shadd Maruna is in the departments of human development and justice studies at Queens University Belfast Law School. He is the author of *Making Good: How Ex-Convicts Reform and*

Rebuild Their Lives (American Psychological Association Books, 2001).

Fergus McNeill is in the department of criminology and social work at the University of Glasgow. He is the co-editor of *Offender Supervision: New Directions in Theory, Research, and Practice* (Willan/Routledge, 2010).

RECOMMENDED READING

Peggy C. Giordano, Stephen A. Cernkovich, and Jennifer L. Rudolph. 2002. "Gender, Crime, and Desistance: Toward a Theory of Cognitive Transformation," *American Journal of Sociology* 107(4):990–1064. Develops a cognitive theory to explain desistance among serious female delinquents as well as their male counterparts.

Megan C. Kurlychek, Robert Brame, and Shawn D. Bushway. 2006. "Scarlet Letters and Recidivism: Does an Old Criminal Record Predict Future Offending?" *Criminology & Public Policy* 5(3):483–504. Shows that the risk of new crimes among those who have desisted for seven years is similar to the risk of new crimes among persons with no criminal record.

John H. Laub and Robert J. Sampson. 2003. *Shared Beginnings, Divergent Lives: Delinquent Boys to Age 70.* Cambridge, MA: Harvard University Press. A classic long-term study of desistance following Boston men from adolescence to old age.

Shadd Maruna. 2001. *Making Good: How Ex-Convicts Reform and Rebuild Their Lives.* Washington, D.C.: American Psychological Association. A pathbreaking desistance study that focuses on narratives of personal change.

Fergus McNeill. 2006. "A Desistance Paradigm for Offender Management," *Criminology and Criminal Justice* 6(1):39–62. A clear and powerful application of desistance theory to criminal justice practice.

TSP tie-in

offender gender

Each year, men commit the vast share of violent crimes in the United States. Even so, as early as the nineteenth century, criminologists feared that the "liberation" of women would release women's violent underbelly, bringing their offending rates in line with (or even beyond) men's rates. One such criminologist, Cesare Lombroso, warned that the "innocuous semi-criminal within all women" would emerge if the "constraints of domesticity and maternity" were released. Criminologists such as Freda Adler echoed this sentiment in the 1960s and '70s, hypothesizing that the women's liberation movement had opened up criminal opportunities for women as well as improved prospects in the home and workplace. The "liberation" hypothesis suggests that as women gain social power and freedoms, they experience fewer informal controls, leading to more opportunities to commit crime and violence. In the '70s, even the U.S. Commission on Causes and Prevention of Violence openly worried over the liberation threat.

Today, there is little evidence to suggest that Women's Lib or nontraditional gender attitudes have increased women's and girls' delinquency or crime. For example, research by Peggy Giordano and Stephen Cernkovich indicates that girls who accept nontraditional female behaviors report *less* delinquent behavior. And, though U.S. arrest rates for women and girls did climb in the 1960s and early '70s, so did arrest rates for men and boys. Moreover, arrest rates may be more indicative of changes in policing policies than women's "liberty" to commit crime. Further, actual incarceration rates show an enormous gender gap. While the Census Bureau reports that women account for 68% of nursing home residents and 54% of college dorm residents, they take up only 9% of prison beds (see graphs comparing gender differentials in group quarters posted at thesocietypages.org/crime).

Estimates based on victimization surveys (rather than arrest data) suggest that the gender gap for violent offenses (aggravated assault, robbery, and simple assault) narrowed slightly between the mid-1970s and 2005. But research by Janet Lauritsen, Karen Heimer, and James Lynch finds it's not because women have become more violent but because women's rates of violence have decreased more slowly than men's in the overall crime drop.

While the gap may not be as wide as it once was, men still commit violent crime at rates far higher than women. This "social fact" raises the question of whether gender-specific theories are needed to explain women's violent offending. Or, as Jody Miller and Christopher Mullins suggest, a more appropriate question may be: "Why *don't* women commit crime?"

SUZY MCELRATH

discussion guide and group activities

1. Chapter 1 discusses how crime has dropped dramatically in recent decades. Browse to thesocietypages.org /crime and read the Public Criminology posts "Okay violence is down, but have *mass* shootings increased?" and "Are we more violent than ever before?" Discuss these U.S. crime trends and what factors might affect our perceptions about the prevalence of the most shocking crimes.

2. Several chapters in *Crime and the Punished* discuss how social institutions influence crime rates. For another example of how one institution, the economy, may affect social behavior, browse to thesocietypages.org/crime to read "Unemployment and Deportation." Choose Chapter 1, 2, or 11 to read alongside this post. How do you think social institutions affect crime or suicide rates? Did your idea of how social institutions relate to crime change after you read the chapter?

3. Chapter 4 illustrates U.S. punishment over the past several decades. List three ways that punishment varies geographically and socially. Drawing on Chapters 4 and 5, list three factors other than crime that might be associated with higher rates of punishment.

4. The authors of Chapters 5, 6, and 10 discuss the role of politics and public opinion in changing punishment policies in the twenty-first century. Discuss two or three ways that these social forces are related.

5. Rosenfeld and Messner discuss in chapter 11 how, in various ways, "smart policing" tactics bring some elements of surveillance and imprisonment into our communities. Click on the NYPD Stop and Frisk graphic at thesocietypages.org/crime and describe how you think this image illustrates or refutes Rosenfeld and Messner's argument.

6. In Chapter 1, the authors suggest that prison may be *criminogenic*. Browse to thesocietypages.org/crime and listen to the Office Hours podcast with Matthew Snodgrass. Why might there be a relationship between the amount of time spent in prison and re-offending, according to Snodgrass? Knowing what you know now, what changes would you suggest so that punishment is less likely to promote further crime?

7. Chapter 12 raises questions about imposing long prison terms for offenses committed by juveniles. Why might

some people support shorter prison sentences for juvenile offenders, even those who have committed murder? Read the post "Murderers & Thieves" at thesocietypages .org/crime. List at least three potential risks and three benefits of policies that take specific offenses, sentence lengths, and age at the time of the crime into account when considering parole. Form groups of two or three to discuss.

8. Chapters 7 and 12, as well as this volume's "Changing Lenses" piece, highlight the social relationships between prisoners and their loved ones. Browse to thesocietypages .org/crime to visit the archive of the "We Are the 1 in 100" project. Choose two photos you find particularly evocative and discuss your choices with others in your reading group.

9. What *is* genocide and what makes genocide a crime, according to Chapter 9? Why do so many people think genocide is unique? Listen to the Office Hours podcast with John Hagan at thesocietypages.org/crime. What does Hagan say is the difference between genocide and crimes against humanity?

10. The International Criminal Court (ICC) has indicted a sitting head of state on charges of genocide, crimes against humanity, and war crimes. List a few reasons why this is remarkable. How might prosecuting these

mass atrocities be different if it is undertaken at the international level rather than in national courts?

featured activity 1: desistance and reentry

How and why people stop committing crime is an important question for social scientists, policymakers, and criminal justice practitioners. Chapter 13 describes how two social scientists "co-created" a film about desistance from the perspective of former prisoners and practitioners who work with them. The film is available to watch online. This activity will help readers think about how policy and practice could better incorporate what we know about the desistance process.

Watch the 50-minute film *The Road From Crime* (click through from thesocietypages.org/crime). As you watch, consider these discussion questions:

1. In what ways might the criminal justice system promote reoffending?
2. According to the filmmakers, desistance is both an internal and external process. How can you see this in their film?
3. What punishment policies or practices could be changed, added, or abandoned to better promote desistance?

4. Most people who work in the criminal justice system have never been convicted of serious crimes. How do you think criminal justice would be different if it had more input from people who had been through the process themselves?

After watching the film, imagine that you are a social worker in a community where many former inmates return after leaving prison (say, a neighborhood of Baltimore or Chicago). What resources would you need to address community needs and help former inmates desist from crime? What community leaders or organizations would you need to enlist for support? Discuss your thoughts with your group.

featured activity 2: responding to mass shootings

For understandable reasons, horrible events such as mass shootings often garner a great deal of media attention, fear, and political outrage. Yet current social scientific knowledge about topics like violence, gun control, and mental illness is frequently obscured or excluded from these reports and calls for action. The following activity can be done individually or as a group and will help readers think about how social scientific evidence could influence policy in this arena.

PART A

Browse the Internet to gather two or three news stories from the weeks following a recent mass shooting in the United States. Use the stories to answer these questions:

1. What claims are made in these stories about the causes of mass shootings?
2. What calls for change are made by victims' families, politicians, experts, or others?
3. What policies are suggested to address mass shootings?

PART B

Read Chris Uggen's Public Criminology post "A Broader-Based Response to Shootings" at thesocietypages.org/crime. With a group of two or three others, discuss the following questions:

1. How does social science evidence compare to media reports?
2. What does the evidence suggest we should be doing to address these crimes?

about the contributors

Hollie Nyseth Brehm is a PhD candidate in the sociology program at the University of Minnesota. She studies human rights, international crime, representations of atrocities, and environmental sociology. She is an NSF Graduate Research Fellow and the graduate editor of The Society Pages.

Joshua Cain is the secretary of the Lifers Club and a college student at the Oregon State Penitentiary.

Deborah Carr is in the sociology department and the Institute for Health, Health Care Policy, and Aging Research at Rutgers University. She is the coauthor of *Introduction to Sociology*, now in its 8th edition (W. W. Norton, 2011).

Megan Comfort is senior research sociologist with the Urban Health Program at RTI International and an assistant adjunct professor at University of California–San Francisco. She is the author of *Doing Time Together: Love and Family in the Shadow of the Prison* (The University of Chicago Press, 2007).

Shannon Golden is a PhD candidate in sociology at the University of Minnesota. She is writing her dissertation on how communities rebuild after violence and human rights violations.

Douglas Hartmann is in the sociology department at the University of Minnesota. His research interests focus on race and ethnicity, multiculturalism, popular culture (including sports and religion), and contemporary American society. He is coeditor of The Society Pages.

Michelle Inderbitzin is in the sociology department at Oregon State University. She regularly teaches Inside-Out classes at the Oregon State Penitentiary.

Sarah Lageson is in the sociology program at the University of Minnesota. She studies media, crime, and law. Sarah is a cohost of the Office Hours podcast.

Suzy McElrath is in the sociology program at the University of Minnesota. She studies the sociology of law and criminology, with a focus on mass atrocity, transitional justice, collective memory, and gender violence.

Steven F. Messner is in the sociology department at the State University of New York at Albany. He is the author, with Richard Rosenfeld, of *Crime and the Economy* (Sage Publications, 2013).

Joshua Page is in the department of sociology at the University of Minnesota. He is the author of *The "Toughest Beat": Politics, Punishment, and the Prison Officers' Union in California* (Oxford University Press, 2011).

Julie A. Phillips is in the sociology department and the Institute for Health, Health Care Policy, and Aging Research at Rutgers University. She studies the causes and consequences of various forms of social inequality, including violent crime, suicide, marital disruption, and migration.

Richard Rosenfeld is in the department of criminology and criminal justice at the University of Missouri–St. Louis. He is a former president of the American Society of Criminology and is the curator of crimetrends.com.

Sarah Shannon is in the department of sociology at the University of Georgia. She studies crime, punishment, and public welfare programs.

Jonathan Simon is at Berkeley Law at the University of California. He is the author of the forthcoming *Mass*

Incarceration on Trial: America's Courts and the Future of Imprisonment (The New Press, 2014).

Christopher Uggen is in the sociology department at the University of Minnesota. He studies crime, law, and deviance, especially how former prisoners manage to put their lives back together. He is coeditor of The Society Pages.

Trevor Walraven is the president of the Lifers Club and a college student at the Oregon State Penitentiary.

index